STRAW MAN

MY BATTLE WITH ANOREXIA

— JACOB ROTH —

STRAW MAN
MY BATTLE WITH ANOREXIA

Copyright © 2018 Jacob Roth.

All rights reserved. No part of this book may be used or reproduced by any means, graphic, electronic, or mechanical, including photocopying, recording, taping or by any information storage retrieval system without the written permission of the author except in the case of brief quotations embodied in critical articles and reviews.

iUniverse books may be ordered through booksellers or by contacting:

iUniverse
1663 Liberty Drive
Bloomington, IN 47403
www.iuniverse.com
1-800-Authors (1-800-288-4677)

Because of the dynamic nature of the Internet, any web addresses or links contained in this book may have changed since publication and may no longer be valid. The views expressed in this work are solely those of the author and do not necessarily reflect the views of the publisher, and the publisher hereby disclaims any responsibility for them.

Any people depicted in stock imagery provided by Getty Images are models, and such images are being used for illustrative purposes only. Certain stock imagery © Getty Images.

ISBN: 978-1-5320-4175-4 (sc)
ISBN: 978-1-5320-4174-7 (e)

Library of Congress Control Number: 2018903330

Print information available on the last page.

iUniverse rev. date: 04/30/2018

To Mom and Dad,

I know that reading this book will be horrible. You'll relive the terror I inflicted upon you. I won't apologize for my illness, but I am sorry I was a cause of your anguish. Never blame yourselves, for I was a con artist, concealing from you the depth of my suffering. I hid the worst elements of my crises to shield you from my torment and give myself the freedom to commit unfettered self-harm. That lifestyle—regardless of how I feel at a given time—no longer appeals to me. I promise I will never deliberately force you to write my obituary. However, if something happens to me, please donate my body to science or an anorexic cannibal.

    I can't control how this book will affect the public perception of our family. But no matter what anybody claims or whether members of Westboro Baptist Church picket with God Hates Anorexics signs outside our house, you must realize that you have been incredible parents. For as long as I can remember, you two have been my best friends (except for when you forced me onto a table and allowed a strange man to hack off something sensitive in front of an audience). That bond will never fracture. I love you. I love our family.

To my sister, Maddie,

I was supposed to be your big brother, but you helped guide me through my vulnerability. You heard more about my pain than anybody else did. I wasn't easy to deal with, yet you never abandoned me. You supported me with levels of maturity and emotional intelligence that far exceeded what someone should expect from a high school student. I'm proud to have such a generous, compassionate, and caring sister. If I were cooler than I am, I'd find a Justin Bieber lyric to express my gratitude to you. Instead, I'm stuck with my words. They'll never suffice.

To Nana Sheila, Zaidy Paul, Bubby Pearl, and Zaidy Jerry,
spending time with my grandparents has never been
a chore. You are all incredible sources of support.

To Gillian Olsen,
your love and encouragement helped me overcome
my doubts and move forward with this project.

To Aunt Bonnie, Aunt Karrie, Aunt Riva, Uncle
Dave, Uncle Richard, Uncle Steve, Alexa, Aaron,
Jared, Justin, Lindsay, Trevor, and Tyler,
many of my best memories include you.

To Adam Kovacs-Litman, Ari Soberano, Katherine Fu,
Lyndsay Lyons, Mathew Sherman, and WuDi Wu,
you all know what you've done for me.

To Darko Ficko,
I love you as if you were my big brother.

To Gillian Kirsh,
you were an ideal collaborator.

To the members of CSA2,
you all gave me one of the best half months of my adolescence.

To Maurizio De Franco,
thank you for nurturing my irreverence.

To Alex Robins, Noah Letofsky, and Sophie Barnett,
we understand one another. Thank you for your
openness and for allowing me to laugh at our pasts.

To Aviva Koffman, Jennifer Goldberg, and John Lambersky,
you introduced me to the fundamentals of writing. Without
your harshness, I wouldn't have been able to write this book.

To Amelia McLeod, Charlie McMahan, Diana Holloway,
Irfan Tahiri, Katrina Dods, Kaya Ellis, Ksenia Podvoiskaia,
Mariana Vitaver, Husein Panju, Jordyn Letofsky,
Julia Kaplan, Pamela Charach, Rebecca Schidlowsky,
Richard Waters, Ryan Tolusso, Stuart Clark, Taylor
Mann, William Gibson, and Zachary Wilson,
you've all helped me more than you may ever realize.

To Norma Kirsh,
throughout this project, your advice has been invaluable.

To Merryl Bear, Suzanne Phillips, and the National
Eating Disorder Information Centre team,
thanks for allowing me to be part of your crew.

To my elementary school principal,
who guaranteed I'd flounder,
you were right. I went ano.

INTRODUCTION

My Lapsed Religion

Anorexia nervosa is like a fanatical religious conviction. You dedicate all your energy to a way of life that you believe promises bliss. The eating disorder ritualizes internal crises that you struggle to understand. My experiences with anorexia were based on rituals that I'd perform to avoid panic. I treated the voice in my head as if it were divine, trying to suppress all skepticism and fully submit to its offerings. That's why I personify it as the Anorexia God. I do this not to make light of religion but to demonstrate the existential purpose I gave to anorexia. I also emphasize the fanatical element. My convictions were dangerous and based on a self-destructive neurosis.

Anorexia is not just a desire to be thin. It is an all-encompassing fear of gaining weight or an obsessive preoccupation with losing weight. To control weight, an anorexic restricts caloric intake. This restriction doesn't amount to healthy dieting. It overtakes the patient's life.

Failure to comply with the Anorexia God's edicts would send me to anorexia hell. If I consumed one calorie too many, ate one gram of fat too many, or weighed one pound too many, I felt I had defied my religious obligation. I was a sinner—a sacrilegious, sodomy-sympathizing heretic.

I wasn't born into this religion, but when I found it, I converted quickly. It answered the unanswerable and controlled the uncontrollable. My unfulfilled needs made this new interpretation of existence alluring. The dictates of my regimen soothed my lost soul, nullifying its contradictions and imperfections. Life made sense.

My friends ask me how a once chubby teenager who acted as if he were a refined adult could have succumbed to this faith. How did a student who excelled to the top of his high school graduating class morph into a gaunt carrier of such pain? How did a guy who was big enough that he had to strain his neck to see the toilet bowl crumble that profoundly? How did people's tutor become a patient who needed everybody's help? How did a man become anorexic?

I still can't answer these questions with certainty. I can only try.

In this book (for which I hope the market isn't too thin), I tell the story of my pilgrimage from a healthy lifestyle to my arrival at recovery. But I offer four points of caution.

First, everything I have written is my interpretation of events and people's reactions to them. It represents just one angle. When I was sick, many of my perceptions were unrealistic. I was sure people hated me, a view that retrospection has undermined. My story describes my thoughts as they occurred. I want you to see how I saw the world.

Second, I claim to tell the story of only one anorexic, for my experiences with an eating disorder aren't universal. Though I've sprinkled this account with advice that I deemed helpful, anguish has diverse origins and manifestations. I am also unqualified to offer professional advice, so I advise reading my text as a memoir.

Third, my recovery was quick and unconventional

(spoiler alert). I didn't seek much professional help. That's why most of my story focuses on my struggle with anorexia rather than my recovery. My goal is to give you a tour of my anorexic mind. If you're looking for a text that's heavy on material about recovery, this book might not be for you.

Fourth, anorexia is a rotten idea. You should eat food.

While the account that follows this introduction is substantively truthful, descriptions of events in the distant past are my best recollections. I have a good memory, but I have not memorized conversations from the '90s.

I have changed some names and minor details about people to protect their anonymity. Publishing the names of adults who were jerks when they were in elementary school would not be proportional justice.

CHAPTER 1

Beginnings

I grew up in a loving family. Born in 1992, I was the first of two children. Maddie joined us three years later. We lived in Toronto, a bustling city that some call the New York of Canada.

My parents, Ellen and Sammy, were never strict. Mom bought me all the stuffed animals I wanted and punished wrongdoing with brief time-outs in my bedroom.

"Did you throw a block at your sister's head again?" Mom would ask.

"Yes. She started it."

"Go to your room."

Until I was fourteen years old, Dad didn't think I could spell.

"Ell," he would say to my mom, "like I said, that lady at the store was being such a d-a-m b-i-t-c-h. F-u-c-k her and her s-h-i-t-y attitude."

"Sam, you know the kids can spell," she'd say. "And *shitty* has two *t*'s in it. *Damn* has an *n*, unless you're talking about a water dam."

Perhaps my father's spellings represented his subconscious yearning for his kids never to grow up. To Dad, each year brought new potential hazards from which he could not protect us. He'd put his hands in his black but graying curls when he sensed danger. In most cases, Dad's nervousness was zany. I didn't always want to zip my jacket up to my neck as if I were a mummy, and Maddie didn't always look both ways nineteen times before crossing a residential street.

Maddie was a rotten kid. When she was two years old, she'd swim in a pool with her water wings on, screaming, "Fuck!" as loudly as she could. She'd lift her skirt in public (despite refusing to wear underwear), throw hard objects at me, jam pebbles in her nose, slam her head against chairs, and break my toys. Her curly black hair was always matted.

Despite the eccentricity, we were a close family. We'd spend a lot of time with my four grandparents. Eventually, we added a Portuguese water dog named Molly to the group.

My family did typical secular Jewish middle-class things. Taking trips to Florida during the winter holidays, spending summer weekends at the cottage, and having Chinese-food dinners on Christmas Eve were staples.

Every characteristic of my childhood should have produced something normal—whatever that means.

But beyond the exterior, I developed a strong self-hatred before my teens. My first recollection of this fixation is from third grade.

Ricky Samuel was my best friend at United Synagogue Day School. We played hockey in each other's driveways at least once a week and learned swear words together.

In third grade, Ricky distanced himself from me and migrated to the school's social elites. He became reluctant to confirm any plans with me. He'd respond to my invitations by telling me he was hanging out with his new crew or would have to wait to see whether anything else came up. At the time, I thought he was bullying me. I was so paranoid that I believed he intended to slight me, as I assumed any decision that affected me was made because of me. My friendship seemed like the minor-league affiliate of a sports team, as its central purpose was to train him for the big show of the social world.

I could have been more assertive and joined Ricky's new crew, but I felt uncomfortable with my presence. My mannerisms seemed awkward and uncoordinated. I wasn't sure when people wanted to talk to me or when I was a nuisance. If someone I barely knew didn't invite me to a small birthday party, I thought the person intended to be hurtful. The reality was that the kids probably knew only my name, as I was shy and usually sat in the back of the class. Most people treated me as they would have a poster on the wall in the school's corridor. They recognized that I existed yet saw me as a space filler rather than anything substantial. Still, I was convinced they should have included me in all their plans.

I'd leave school and complain to my parents and grandparents about what I thought was poor treatment, embellishing most of my stories to provoke grand compliments. They'd tell me I was special, the other kids were jealous of me, and I was handling the situation with the utmost maturity.

Internalizing this constant praise made me think that everyone else should have treated me as if I were a superstar.

One incident at overnight camp encapsulated this dissonance.

It was a hot evening in early July 2004. The mosquitoes swarmed like attacking armies, and a humid breeze sprayed the camp's buildings with dust it picked up from the ground. I was a plump kid lying alone on the top bunk in the corner of a wooden cabin. My cabinmates were not going to return to their summer dwelling until the 9:30 p.m. curfew, which was just more than an hour away. They were mingling with the rest of the inhabitants. Laughs and screams of teenagers filled the cinnamon-bun-scented air. "Did you guys kiss?" I heard a muffled voice say in the distance.

"Hell nah, dude. Her? That chick? Really? No freaking way, man. Not a chance. She's basically a fucking man, yo," another faceless person responded. This voice was unmistakable. It was Bobby Tucker, the leader of the cabin and the camper whose persona I wished I could have adopted for the summer. Everyone listened to whatever he said, followed him wherever he went, and laughed at his flat jokes. Nobody called him Bobby; he was Bobby Tucker, a brand name at camp. His friendship admitted one into the upper echelons of the popularity hierarchy or at least was a ticket to social relevance.

Like an exhausted dog, I curled into a ball on my bed and slammed my head into my knees. I flicked the switch on my yellow pocket-sized portable radio and listened to the sports updates. I thought I was useful to my peers solely because of my always-up-to-date knowledge of National Hockey League news.

There wasn't any news that night, so I left my bunk to turn off the lights and go to sleep. However, when I reached the front of the cabin, a crazed older camper burst into my quarters and drenched me with a few trigger pulls of his water gun. He disappeared into a crowd of hysterical teenagers.

"You should have seen the look on his face, yo!" he yelled. "He was so stunned. Totally fucking stunned, yo. Ha!"

I changed my shirt and returned to my bunk. Pictures of my black-and-white Portuguese water dog, Molly, hung above my bed. They reminded me that the end of July would bring a return to those who cared about me. Because I had so many images of my dog, my cabinmates called me Doggy Style, a nickname I accepted without understanding the innuendo behind it. In a letter to my parents, I wrote, "When I get home, call me Doggy Style instead of Jake. That's what all of my fellow campers call me." Mom and Dad must have been confused.

I tried to turn on the radio for one final check on the sporting universe, but the device didn't react. After four attempts to change its batteries, it still failed. Without the radio, I would be irrelevant. I panicked and ran through all my violations of coolness: the air ball I'd shot on the basketball court, my silence during a group hangout the evening before, and my failure to participate in the midsession dance. Waves of disappointment drowned my head. I believed I was too awkward for my contemporaries to accept. *How do I stand? What do I do with my right hand to keep it from dangling foolishly? What is the proper way to sit? Is there a correct way to eat? What is a suitable conversation topic?* I feared my inability to answer these questions that I pondered nightly. How was I going to reverse so many years of social futility?

I smashed the radio against the wall, swinging until it broke into sharp chunks.

My pillow was soaked with tears, my nose was leaking, and my right palm was bleeding from the jagged edges of the radio's plastic. I could not catch my breath, for my self-lambasting would not cease. Amid a soundtrack of exuberance, I lay alone in my bed, trapped inside the prison of my mind.

The cabin's door slammed open, the lights turned on, and a sweaty group of kids bolted in. I don't think they noticed me, as my head remained ensconced in the mattress and my body was buried under the scratchy comforter. Until the on-duty staff member demanded, "Lights out," rap music was blasting. My cabinmates were throwing tennis balls against rafters, eating sugary candy, and talking about the latest gossip. Nobody came near my bed. Within a couple of hours, I was the only one awake.

Soon a few members of the camp's water-ski staff tiptoed into our cabin and covered us in shaving cream. Most of the guys in my cabin thought the prank was funny, but I was unable to see the humor in it. I was going to have to change my sheets and use more clothes.

Those nuisances didn't seem to bother the cabinmates I aspired to resemble. I wanted to be more like them. So I planned to act like the water-ski staff the next night.

Huntsville was a sauna again. The evening program, a camp-wide play, had just finished, and we had forty-five minutes until we had to be in the cabin. Underneath a pink sky, my age group congregated in a circle on the main field. Bobby Tucker led a discussion about his disdain for our unit head, Sammy. "He's such a buzzkill. I fucking hate that guy, you know." Chaim, Thomas, Vanessa, Jennifer, Sarah, and Sophia all agreed and added new reasons to support Bobby Tucker's opinion.

I took an audibly deep breath, as doubt was consuming my brain. *Come on, Jake. Say something. It's going to be stupid. Say something. It won't be that bad. Anything. You'll sound like an idiot. Do you like Sammy? Yeah, you do. But who cares?*

"Um, I hate swim class," I said.

They turned to look at me but didn't acknowledge that

I had said anything. I was a chirping bird, heard rather than noticed, both present and absent. Their discussion continued uninterrupted and unaffected by what I had said. I walked back to the cabin.

After the remaining campers returned and fell asleep, I began the second phase of my plan. Part one, joining a conversation, had been unsuccessful, so I needed the other half of the strategy to be fruitful. I removed a pack of pens and markers from my duffel bag and left my bunk. Everybody was snoring, and Peter was talking in his sleep. "I don't like broccoli and spinach," he mumbled.

I approached Alex's bed and drew a brown mustache on his face. Bobby Tucker got a happy face. Simon's chin had polka dots on it. Chaim received black lines like the ones football and baseball players wear. I drew a penis with two heads on Thomas's chin, and I covered Jonathan's forehead in blue streaks. Within five minutes, I had redesigned all of my cabinmates' faces. I went to sleep feeling satisfied.

The next morning, Bobby Tucker awoke incensed. "Who the fuck drew all over my face?" he said.

Everyone else was similarly enraged.

"I'm going to kill that motherfucker," Jonathan said. "What kind of fucking idiot would do that?"

"It was me, guys," I admitted, giggling nervously. "I thought it would be funny. You don't like it?"

"No, we definitely don't fucking like it, you sick piece of shit. Fucking creep," Simon said. "What the hell is wrong with you, dude?"

I didn't understand their anger. What was the difference between my joke and the water-ski staff's shaving cream prank from the night before?

"Are you insane?" Chaim asked. "Like, are you?"

"You're dead tonight," Gavin said. "Dead, Roth."

"You're a moron, Roth!" Jonathan screamed.

I was dizzy and nauseated. I wanted to cry but would not show such weakness in front of the guys, so I apologized and left early for the dining hall. On the way there, I sat on a boulder, put my face in my palms, and allowed myself to indulge in some self-pity. I wanted to vanish.

"Fuck you, Jake," I heard in the background. "Piece-of-shit bitch."

I flinched.

At breakfast, I offered to refill all the empty muffin and pancake trays. I cleaned the table. I wiped up any spills. I returned all the utensils to the kitchen. After I left the dining hall, I went to the cabin for cleanup. I did all the chores. I swept the floor. I folded all the clothes on the clothesline outside. I scrubbed the toilets and the sink. I made the beds. I took out the garbage.

My contrition didn't lead to relief.

"We're going to get you back a million times worse tonight, Jake," Bobby Tucker said above echoing voices.

"How could you do something so fucked up to your own cabin? Seriously," Chaim said. "That's so low, man—very fucking low."

I apologized as if I had killed somebody, yet nobody accepted my sincerity. Or they didn't care that I was sorry. That night, after lights-out, I snuck out of my cabin and ran for five minutes until I was deep in the secluded woods, where I sat on twigs in the dirt with my legs crossed. I thought about all the praise my family threw at me. Did they mean it? Was I really intelligent? Did I have that much value? Were they dishonest to make me love myself? Or did they have to say those things out of familial obligation?

I sobbed until I could see the sun popping out from behind the black curtain in the sky. Images of once repressed sources of sadness rushed through my consciousness. I saw the lonely weekend nights on which I would sit at home by myself and drink juice boxes in my bed. I saw the solitary lunchtimes when I was around people but was alone. I saw myself unable to stand in a way that didn't make me look awkward, and I saw my athletic incompetence and fear of participating in gym class. I concluded that I'd spent the first decade of my childhood alone in a forest. The salty tears burned my bloodshot eyes.

For the first time in my life, I wanted to die.

CHAPTER 2

Jebediah in Susej, Maryville

My self-diagnosed social uselessness extended into my high school years. I'd panic about how even my closest friends perceived me.

I waited for people to talk to me at the few parties I went to. I was so proper that many of my peers referred to me as a seventy-year-old inside a kid's body.

The alcohol-soaked basement party that Sarah Weinberg held at the beginning of my eleventh grade exemplified my discomfort around my peers. I didn't want to attend, but my mother encouraged me to go.

"You should get out, Jake. It won't kill you to have some fun," she said.

"I really don't want to."

"Just go. It won't be so bad. I'll help you out and pick up a gift card to the mall for Sarah's birthday."

I agreed to attend because I didn't want to argue. Mom bought the gift card that I'd give to Sarah.

I slipped on a black Under Armour hoodie and blue jeans before driving to Sarah's house. A ten-minute drive passed in what felt like thirty seconds.

I approached the door as if I were walking barefoot on hot coals and took a deep breath before ringing the bell.

Sarah opened the door within a few seconds. "Hey! So good to see you," she said, slurring her words.

Sarah showed me to the packed basement, where inebriated teenagers were wetting the carpet with their beverages.

The basement was spacious. A home gym with leather mats, an exercise bike, a treadmill, and a weight bench filled an alcove on the opposite side of the winding staircase leading to the basement. A sliding glass door that connected to the backyard comprised most of the gym's adjacent wall. I felt as if the low ceilings were descending toward my head.

In the middle of the basement, Ashley and Gretchen were checking for lumps and taste-testing each other's saliva. Bernard was attempting a fourth keg stand. Raquel and Brian, the school's unlikeliest and most troubled couple, were arguing loudly. Samantha and Sari were texting each other from the same bench. Hailey, who had just left the bathroom after spending at least half an hour in it, had dried vomit on the bottom left corner of her chin's pasty white skin.

For more than two hours, I circled the basement, wishing somebody would talk to me. I moved with the obscurity of a Roomba vacuum. You could have stubbed your toe on me.

I sat down beside Raquel and Brian, who had moved to a black linen sofa dotted with crumbs of recently eaten potato chips.

All right, Jake. Work up the courage to say something to them.

"Great party, eh?" I said.

"Yeah, man, great party," Brian said, turning his attention from Raquel. "Lots of good potential men for you here, Roth."

"Men?"

"Yeah, there are lots of good eligible bachelors."

"Not that there is anything wrong with that kind of lifestyle, but I'm not gay. I respect that there are a multiplicity of sexual preferences, but I'm heterosexual."

"Really? Hmm, I always thought you were a gay, dude. My bad."

"It's no problem. Do you think you're ready for the test on *Everyman*?"

"Yeah, the test shouldn't be that bad. S'all good."

Raquel was silent.

"What's your favorite class this year?" I asked.

"I don't know, man. It's school. They're all kinda the same."

"Jake." Tim, who was charging the sofa with the enthusiasm of a participant in the Gloucestershire Cheese Rolling, interrupted. "Come here for a sec. Leave them alone on the couch." He took a sip of Corona from a glass bottle.

"Why?"

"Are you serious?"

"Yeah, why?"

"He's trying to hook up with her, and you're being a major cock block."

Embarrassed about my obliviousness, I obeyed.

Tim returned to the friends he had left to reprimand me.

I continued to roam the basement, feeling as if I were a monk at a sex club. Everybody else seemed to fit into place. The others had the confidence and wherewithal to pursue their sources of happiness.

At midnight, I was ready to leave.

"Jake!" Ashley called from a few feet away. "Do you think you could drive Gretchen and me home?"

I had a reputation for being a designated driver. Everyone

knew I had a car and was under the influence only of my weirdness. I was happy to feel wanted.

"Of course I can give you a ride. What time were you thinking of leaving?"

"Around two. Does that sound legit?"

"That's when I was thinking of leaving too, so that's totally cool."

I became a citizen of the weight bench over the next two hours. Partiers briefly joined me to rest their feet or recover from nausea, but beyond pleasantries, I never engaged them. I studied my waterproof Timex watch, counting the minutes until I could escape that basement and watching everything that I wanted to be. I would have traded academic intelligence for the ability to interact meaningfully with my cohorts.

I thought about driving my car into a lake but rejected the idea because of the environmental damage it would cause. Those thoughts erased time. The movement of people blurred into a monolith of colors and shapes.

"All right, Jake, we're ready to go," Ashley announced at two fifteen.

"To where am I taking you?" I asked Ashley.

"We're going to Newmarket."

I didn't care that Newmarket was forty-five minutes out of the way from my house. For that level of attention, I would have driven anywhere.

Ashley and Gretchen sat in the back seat of my car. They were like twins. Both had long dyed-black hair, light brown skin, and small noses. They wore white jeans that fit tightly against their average builds and blue denim buttoned shirts.

When we reached the highway, they again quenched their thirst by gulping each other's saliva. They were moaning, grunting, and making sucking noises. When I turned my head to check my blind spot, I could see Gretchen caressing Ashley's petite breasts.

"I hope you can keep this between us," Gretchen said to me as she reached inside Ashley's bra. "We haven't come out, but like, we're gay."

"Really? You've hidden it so well."

"That's good. We were worried we were a tad too PDA at the party."

"Too PDA? I mean, I don't think anybody would have figured anything out."

"That's good."

Gretchen and Ashley returned to kissing. They paused when I drove over a speed bump but then continued until I pulled up to Ashley's house.

"You're home," I had to tell them.

They didn't react to my announcement.

"Hey, um, you're home," I said, clearing my throat. "This is the place where you live, isn't it?"

"Oh yeah, we are," Gretchen responded, putting her tongue back in her mouth and moving her disheveled hair back into place. "Thanks for the ride, Jake. Like, please don't mention our relationship or what you've seen to others."

"I wouldn't dream of it. Have a good night. Don't forget to wash your hands. There were a lot of people sneezing at the party."

Ignoring my joke, they exited the car and made out on the front steps as I drove away. I turned on the radio to pretend I wasn't alone on my trip home.

"We're going to go to Mike in San Antonio, Texas," the radio host said. "Mike, tell us about your experiences with angels and the Holy Spirit."

"Well, I was playing tennis, and I used to have a really, really bad shoulder. I couldn't serve because my rotator cuff was basically just finished. There was such incredible pain. Then, one day, I thought, *You know what? I'm going to try serving. Maybe it will hurt like a mother, but I'm gonna do it.* Next thing y'all know, I felt the touch of an angel on my shoulder. I could feel its breath, its scent—its everything. And I served the ball like I was in my twenties again."

"Praise! Praise be to him!" the host said. "Thanks for the call. Lines are wide open. Give us a shout."

I wanted to distract myself from my failure at the party. One way I knew how to do that was by making myself laugh. This coping mechanism might have brought out some of my worst qualities, but it helped get me through the negative emotions.

That night, I called into the radio show and concocted a ludicrous story.

"We're going to go to Jebediah in Susej, Maryville," the host said, referring to my alias and made-up location. "Jebediah, what's your comment on this beautiful, holy evening?"

"Shabbat Shalom, y'all," I said.

I was trying to focus on the prank call, yet images of myself standing alone in the corner of Sarah's basement were creeping into my mind.

"Ah, do we have a Jewish friend with us?" the host asked.

"Why would you assume I am Jewish?" I was holding back laughter.

"My apologies. You are absolutely correct. Please, go right ahead with your call."

"I was twelve years old, and I found a pubic hair on the floor of my bathroom. I wondered where this little curly thing came from," I said in the tone of a televangelist. "Was my little brother, Avi, bikini-waxing in my bathroom again? And then the thing talked to me. It said, 'Jebediah,

I am the Holy Spirit of the Lord Almighty. I grant you life. Hallelujah.' I was so shocked. I could not pick up the pubic hair, as it weighed about seven hundred fifty pounds. But Lord Almighty, when I touched it, my hands started tingling. I fell to the floor and started convulsing. The Holy Spirit traveled from my feet all the way up to my left earlobe and then back down to the right quadrant of my left testicle. That was the night I found it all. Thank you for taking my call."

"And thank you for making the call, my brother. That's a very unique story."

When the call disconnected, one thought dominated my mind. On a Friday night, I had attended a party with more than one hundred people, yet the single prolonged conversation I'd held was under a fake name with a talk show host who was tripping on LSD.

I exited the highway and pulled into a fast food restaurant, where I ordered four extra-large boxes of fries and a soda. I was trying to freeze the sadness with sodium, hydrogenated oil, and sugar. Overlooking that I was treating my arteries like a gas station bathroom, I shoved the shit into my mouth until it vanished. Then I ordered another extra-large box of fries for the ride home. I ate the fries separately from the seven individual ketchup packets that I squeezed onto my tongue. I wanted to give myself a stomachache to numb the pain of my perceived inability to interact with my peers.

Eventually, I walked out of the restaurant feeling full, and I regretted eating excessive food. I unlocked the car and slammed the driver's-side door upon reentering. The sound of the car starting was irritating. It reminded me that I had exhausted all my stops for the night. I was going home in failure.

I fantasized about smashing the rearview mirror, which displayed the deserted main roads. They paralleled the emptiness I was feeling. The night out had been futile. I'd left with the hope that the script would be different. Upon reaching my house in the early morning, the positivity had choked on its foolishness.

After changing into my Toronto Maple Leafs pajama bottoms and a black T-shirt that read "Fuck you, you fucking fuck," I plastered my face in a pillow, cried, and screamed as quietly but as passionately as I could.

I tried to interrupt the distortions by reminding myself that I had friends.

I thought about Ari Soberano, my closest confidant in middle and high school. Unlike me, he was a local celebrity. When he and I would walk the halls before school started, I marveled at the ridiculous number of people he had to greet. I believed that Ari should have seen me as a sidekick unworthy of his friendship, but he never treated me as such. He knew about the source of my anxiety, the enervating perception that I was Yao Ming at a Little People of America convention. There were not—and still aren't—any boundaries to what we would share with each other.

I also spent many nights in the basements of many friends. We'd watch hockey, play ministicks, and discuss the insignificant problems of adolescence.

Despite those relationships, I felt incapable of interacting with more than one person at a time. Group social settings overwhelmed me.

I was also convinced that my friends pitied me. In my view, they saw me as a burden who was so broken that ending their friendships with me would have been negligent. I would respond to positivity by telling myself that my friends had fabricated it, for they couldn't enjoy the company of someone as socially awkward as I thought I was.

The room alternated between spinning and stillness. I wanted to go home, but I was home. I wanted to be alive, but I was living. I wanted sight, but I could see. I wanted to wake up from my consciousness.

CHAPTER 3

30/45/15

That self-hatred was still prominent when I became a vegetarian in April 2010. I'd felt guilty about eating animals, yet I'd been too lazy to act on my beliefs. Videos of slaughters finally persuaded me I needed to commit myself to a new lifestyle.

"I'm going vegetarian," I told my dad.

"No, you're not. Don't be silly, Jake." He placed his open palms on his head of curly gray hair. Dad's biceps busted through his plain white T-shirt.

"No, really, I am going to do it," I said.

"So you're becoming a vag-atarian? I never thought you were gay—not that there'd be anything wrong with that if you were. This news isn't really a surprise then. Vag-atarian."

Mom, who was in Florida at the time, worried about how I'd get protein.

"Don't worry," I said to her over the phone. "I have a plan in place and have researched how to ensure that I remain healthy. Vegetables are definitely key."

"You? Vegetables? You know that potatoes aren't a vegetable? They're a starch. You haven't really eaten a vegetable other than romaine lettuce covered in creamy Caesar dressing. That doesn't count. Sorry. Come on, Jake.

Be realistic. Maybe go with free range. I've heard all about it. Research it. You don't need to be so extreme."

"I'm not being extreme."

"You're always extreme. You have to do everything ten steps farther than everyone else. Admit it. Is there something else behind this decision? Are you trying to prove a point?"

"No, I believe in this. Look, I know I haven't liked vegetables, but if I eat them, I could acquire a taste. I could also eat things I don't like. Will that take some work and gustatory fortitude? Sure it will. That doesn't mean I'm going to ignore the challenge."

My mother didn't seem to understand that telling me I couldn't do something made me work much harder at accomplishing it. She paused before speaking again. "Okay, please make sure you actually have a plan. Now that you've made such a big change, you'll have to really be careful about what you eat and avoid having bread and starch all the time. You could become really unhealthy and malnourished if you do that."

I wasn't lying about my plan to work on my diet. Becoming vegetarian was also going to be an opportunity to improve my health. I cut out sugary drinks and processed junk, replacing them with lentils, quinoa, protein shakes, and other plant-based foods.

The first few weeks were challenging. I spit out my first bite of a salad with raw vegetables, decorating the plate with a combination of chewed spinach, red pepper, microgreens, and wads of saliva. But I was determined to finish the dish of healthiness and to train myself to enjoy such meals.

I hired a trainer, Darko, to help turn an uncoordinated blob into a nonathletic athlete.

For as long as I've known Darko, he's looked the opposite of what you'd expect from a trainer, let alone one with a name as imposing as Darko. He's as lean as a greyhound and eats jelly beans to recover from workouts. Darko describes himself as "an everyday, ordinary beanpole." In contrast to his name, his skin is very white. Darko almost always wears a baseball cap, a black dry-fit sweater, and black track pants that expose the leanness of his legs. When he works out on the stationary bike or the StairMaster, he pushes himself beyond the point of puking. He goes through one pair of cross-training shoes per year, an attrition rate he attributes to dripping-sweat-induced decay. "I like to suffer," he'll say. "I don't know any other way."

His workouts have unique names. They aren't "chest day" or "leg day." Darko gives protocols his own titles. "Okay, today we are going to light your ass on fire like it's a Christmas tree at a Hanukkah party."

Darko's demeanor is the opposite of his intense training methods. He is gentle and soft-spoken. When I first met Darko, we bonded over pointing out the absurdity of the fitness industry.

"Jeez," I said before we started working out. "Everyone has some magic formula for getting fit."

"Oh fuck, dude, tell me about it. If you touch yourself with your left hand on a Tuesday at 12:02 p.m., you'll look like a fucking Greek god," he said, his arms swaying. "At the end of the day, you have to do the work. There's no magic to it. You have to do the fucking work."

"Seriously."

"All these people demonize sugar. I mean, fuck. If you sit on your ass and do nothing all day, don't eat sugar. But before or after a workout, it's fucking fuel. It's not the devil."

My first few sessions with Darko were shocking. After instructing me on how to do a proper lunge, Darko gave up and let me practice with horrible form until I naturally progressed into being able to do half a lunge. All my movements in the gym looked spastic, yet under Darko's guidance and encouragement that I could "get stronger than [my] wimpy dad," I transformed myself from pathetic to semi-pathetic.

I also began working with a nutritionist, Melissa. She advocated balancing protein, carbohydrates, and fat. An appropriate meal, she advised, "should have around thirty grams of protein, forty-five grams of carbs, and fifteen grams of fat."

Melissa explained, "These three macronutrients work together and need each other. If you have too many carbs, notably simple carbs, your body will burn through them very quickly, and you'll find yourself getting hungry really soon after a meal. If you keep these in balance, you should start to notice major changes in how you look and feel."

With an orthodox mindset that she never proposed, I accepted her advice. The formula 30/45/15 was supposed to be a general guideline, but to me, it was a new law. I weighed everything I ate, and I'd sneak food into restaurants to guarantee that every dish was as close to balanced as it could be.

"Are you putting actual shit in your pasta?" my cousin Lindsay once asked me at a posh restaurant where we were celebrating a family milestone.

I was putting tempeh, a fermented soy product, in my *agnolotti pomodoro*. "No, no, it's just tempeh," I told her.

"That looks so nasty."

She was right, but I didn't care what it looked like.

I loved the combination of getting in shape and altering my diet. The natural weight loss that followed was addicting, especially because it allowed me to wear tight shirts at social gatherings. I'd soak in compliments and questions about my weight-loss strategy.

The ability to regulate how I presented myself to the world seemed like the most fundamental form of strength. Bodily domination substituted for the lack of power in all other spheres of my life. I couldn't control how others viewed me or the disappointment of social failure, but my new diet allowed me to determine my mass.

I had never before considered the physical realm as a potential source of control. I'd always thought about ways to improve my self-worth, a subordinate of how I perceived my peers' perceptions of me. What if that didn't matter? What if I could find a new basis for satisfaction? What if I cared just about how much I weighed? Maybe I needed to achieve supremacy over my body before I could shift attention to my mind.

The kitchen and the gym became my sanctuaries, as I solved complex math equations at the table and worked out almost daily. As the pounds fell from my body, I worried about what would happen when my mass ceased declining.

My streams of consciousness would resemble something like this: *Okay, Jake, you need to run on the treadmill for half an hour and then use the elliptical for twenty-six minutes. After that, do four sets of lunges and jump rope. When you've completed the workout, you can have one cup of lentils. That's eighteen grams of protein, forty grams of carbs, and one gram of fat. Throw in an ounce of hemp seeds. That takes you to twenty-eight grams of protein, fourteen grams of fat, and forty-two on the carbs. Would a cup of raw broccoli work? That's three grams of protein and six carbs. Nope, that would bring you to forty-eight grams of carbs and thirty-one protein. Three cups of raw spinach? That's thirty-one grams of protein and forty-five carbs. Too much protein. So do two cups of raw spinach, which would be thirty protein and forty-four carbs. Then add two tablespoons of kelp. There's your forty-five grams of fat. Now you need an extra gram of fat, so have two almonds. Ah. There you go. 30/45/15.*

Weighing myself became a morning ritual. I'd wake up, urinate, use my parents' bathroom when they weren't in it, record the number on a spreadsheet, and then check the mirror in my bathroom to evaluate my appearance.

The images I saw were never satisfying. There were too many flabby parts. My stomach wasn't flat, and my chest had man boobs. I'd jump up and down, watching my fat bounce in step with my movements.

I figured I was a work in progress.

CHAPTER 4

The Baptism

I remember the day I decided to become anorexic. At that point, my routine wasn't working. My weight hadn't changed in more than a month, even though I was following my 30/45/15 protocol. The fifteen pounds I'd lost hadn't taken away the flab.

It was late in the evening on July 17, 2010.

I was at the family cottage, where most of my favorite childhood memories took place. The cottage is a paneled white aluminum bungalow on Lake Simcoe, about one hour outside of Toronto. On the roadside, a brick path follows a winding concrete driveway leading to a stained beige wooden deck. Two large rectangular windows with black shutters flank a storm door. The side of the cottage facing the lake has three sliding glass doors and a two-level stained wooden deck. Some fifty yards beyond the deck is a dock made of rotting wood and kept in place with steel. Inside, uncountable tchotchkes rattle as you walk on the light brown hardwood floor.

I was in the glass-enclosed shower and scanning a body that I hated. When I rubbed the soap against my belly, I was clutching blubber. As I scrubbed my face, I felt the chubby cheeks that people used to pinch. I thought that "Aw, you have such cute cheeks" was a euphemism for "Aw, you have such a fat face."

The 30/45/15 was over. I needed to cut my intake drastically. There was no other way. I was already consuming fewer calories than I should have been and wasn't adding muscle, despite my frequent strength and hypertrophy workouts. Further reductions would constitute a borderline case of anorexia and would become insufficient. My weight would plateau, and I'd need to eliminate more food again. I'd have to cut calories whenever my weight plateaued.

The anorexia would give me the control I desired. It would make me likeable and increase my confidence to interact with others at those lousy basement parties. Weight was my scapegoat for the social futility I felt powerless to correct.

I drew a horse's penis on the glass door to procrastinate from planning my anorexia. However, I soon wiped away the drawing to compile a list of the next day's meals and approximated their calories:

> Breakfast: 1 large apple—50 calories
>
> Lunch: 1 cup of cooked spelt pasta with a tablespoon of hemp seeds—300 calories
>
> Dinner: 3/4 cup of lentils and quinoa—150 calories
>
> Total: 500 calories

While Mom and Dad's pressure to eat more was going to be challenging, I decided I'd either have to openly defy them (which was undesirable) or lie about the amounts I had eaten when they were not around (which was less undesirable than the previous option). I knew that my new lifestyle would terrify my parents, but I also worried that I could no longer hide the unending feeling of doom I was carrying. If I didn't become anorexic, my pain would be evident, and my parents wouldn't understand why I was down so frequently. On the flip side, becoming anorexic would allow me to remain outwardly cheery. Mom and Dad would worry about the immediate damage, yet they wouldn't see my pain. I created a false dichotomy in which anorexia seemed to be the lone possible cure for my depression. That night in the shower, I chose anorexia.

The medical community sometimes argues that anorexics lack self-awareness. Patients don't recognize that they look emaciated and have warped images of their bodies. This claim did not apply to me. I simultaneously saw fatness and understood that my senses were off. The scale presented objective evidence that I wasn't overweight, but my eyes told me the opposite. In some respects, my obsession with weight loss was like a drug addiction. The addict knows that the drug can kill, but the pleasure of the high is too tempting to ignore.

I grasped that my new routine would endanger my health and could kill me before my nineteenth birthday. But the eating disorder offered a reward I couldn't find anywhere else: control. Like a zealot embarking on a treacherous pilgrimage, I was ready to sacrifice my physical well-being in the name of sacrosanct serenity.

I was choosing this adventure. I wasn't remorseful about the need to lie to my parents, for they couldn't have spotted the depressive alternative to my anorexia. I was protecting them from a brain that a parent would never want to encounter in a child.

Only Molly witnessed my rawest moments. She knew that the best way to numb the torment was to burp in my face or demand that I throw a ball for her to fetch. One Friday night in the spring of ninth grade, I slammed my face in some pillows and tried to fall asleep by eight thirty after I embarrassed myself in school. I'd scored 70 percent on a quiz because I'd mistakenly skipped a multiple-choice question, which meant my responses on the answer sheet didn't match their corresponding questions. I didn't care that the quiz was worth maybe one one-millionth of my overall mark. The stakes didn't determine the internal magnitude of failure. My thoughts were too dark to sleep.

Sixty pounds of dog stepped on my chest and dropped a slobbery yellow ball on my face. She barked and whined until I flicked the ball off the bed and onto the floor, where she could chase it. Then she kicked my hand with her paw to tell me she wanted to wrestle. I obliged. When the game ended thirty minutes later, Molly, her tongue hanging almost down to the sheets, sat down in front of my feet, looking back at me as if she were saying, "See, you dummy? I'm here. Life is fun if you make people want to play with you rather than waiting for them to come to you." Molly was the best therapist I ever visited during my adolescence.

But when the playful distractions were over, my mentality returned to gloominess. I felt inadequate, like a forgettable, awkward blob without any distinguishing characteristics. Until my final few months of high school, weight was never part of my inferiority complex. My discovery of weight loss through the 30/45/15 protocol ignited the possibility of extracting any utility that might have been dormant within me. It made my desire for control attainable by giving me a plan with measurable targets. I believed that July 17, 2010, was my life's first day of genuine clarity, a baptism into the sanctuary of my eventual demise.

"You're doing the right thing," a lower octave of my voice said.

That voice would assume a negative position during internal debates about my self-worth. I now call it the Anorexia God, as it was a divine cheerleader in my head who encouraged my religious awakening. It could both tear me down and put me back together. I'd heard its thoughts in the past, but this time, they had a clear vision.

The Anorexia God built straw man after straw man.

In logic, a straw man is a reasoning error that occurs when someone purposely misrepresents another person's argument to make it easier to defeat. For example, if I said I disliked *Romeo and Juliet*, a straw man response may go like this: "Jake doesn't believe in romance."

The Anorexia God partook in the same kind of thing. He'd twist any claims that contrasted with the anorexic objectives, just as he did that night while I was in the shower.

"You're on the right path, Jake. You can do this," the Anorexia God said. "Whether you resist or lie to your parents doesn't matter as long as you're eating less and less all of the time, okay? Do you want to listen to your parents?"

"Yes and no. I want to salvage the relationship."

"Clearly then, you don't care about taking back control of your life. Your health means nothing to you."

"It does. You're right. I understand."

The hot shower water bounced off my body.

"That's very good. Nobody else gets you. They can't see the hurt, the hidden sadness behind the smile, as I can. You're on your way to becoming a real man. You have no idea how great you're going to feel when the results become more and more pronounced. The cure is on your plate. Well, it's really off your plate."

"I'll wind up getting really sick soon, no?"

"Of course you'll get sick. That's inevitable. Your ability to conquer the pain, to not let it hinder your ultimate objective, is where you'll find the most control. Don't give in to hunger, dizziness, nausea, and exhaustion. They are obstacles. Run through them like they're linebackers."

"That's my goal."

"Good, man. Now, wipe the list off the glass, dry yourself off, get dressed, and go meet your family at the table. Make sure you eat a very, very small portion tonight."

I turned off the water and obeyed the Anorexia God. My mind went silent.

The next afternoon, I followed the guidelines on the shower's glass: I ate three-fourths of a cup of lentils and quinoa for approximately 150 calories.

Mom worried that my meal was too small.

"Jake, are you just going to eat that tiny plate of lentils and quinoa?" she asked.

She sat down at the kitchen table and adjusted her shoulder-length brown hair. Mom was wearing a typical outfit: black pants with a band T-shirt.

"Well, I'm not going to eat the plate," I said. "That would be pretty gross, but yeah, I had a protein bar like an hour ago, so I'm not that hungry."

Mom did a double take of the plate. "That's not enough. I'm concerned about you. With all the working out you're doing, you need to eat more."

"Don't worry. I'm eating plenty. My body is trying to

adjust to combining exertion and the new diet. I'll find the right balance. It may take time. You should see what my abs look like. I could be in a magazine—modeling socks."

"You look great. Don't be so hard on yourself. And please be careful. If you want to see Melissa again, I can arrange that."

"I'll be all right for now. I probably eat like twenty-five hundred calories a day. I eat small meals since they're easier to digest than large portions."

"No, you don't. That's a lie."

"I'm telling you. I do."

Mom threw her palms up in the air and relented. She sighed loudly.

"You see? Lying to your parents is not that difficult," the Anorexia God said.

"It's not difficult now. It will become more complicated once I look half the size of a marathon runner."

"You'll deal with that at the appropriate time. Be happy right now. You're actually onto something for the first time in your life."

After the meal, I lifted my shirt and stared at my belly. It remained abominable to me, yet I found comfort in my solution. I opted to become a fanatic.

When life gives you lemons, eat them because they're low in calories.

I was proud to be anorexic.

CHAPTER 5

Epileptic Fish

Darko noticed that despite weekly weight training, I was shedding weight as if I had given up steroids. I can recall my final pre-university-departure session with Darko. I didn't eat before the 3:00 p.m. appointment, and for more than two weeks, I hadn't exceeded 425 daily calories, surpassing the goal I'd written on the shower glass at the cottage.

"Your dad tells me that you're not eating very much," Darko said, leaning against the wall near the men's changing room door. "What did you have before you came in today?"

"I had a couple of veggie dogs, a large salad, and lentil soup."

He detected my dishonesty. "Okay, Mr. Veggie Dog, Salad, and Lentil Soup, let's see you do some lunges."

I stepped my right foot forward into a lunge, but as I lowered my body, I fell sideways. Two of the other trainers in the small studio were watching me attempt a simple exercise. Three years later, Darko told me he'd asked them to observe my lunges because he had never before seen anybody so uncoordinated and wondered whether somebody else would have an idea about how to improve the connection between my brain and limbs.

I tried it again, this time stepping with my left foot. My body fell sideways.

"Rather than going all the way down, just go as deep as you can without falling," Darko said.

"You like when your clients go down and deep with you, don't you, Darko?"

Darko and I had developed a rapport based on shock humor.

"Do the lunges, you sick fuck," Darko said. "I can't believe I'm even engaging you in this conversation."

The movements that followed resembled more of a drunken curtsy than a lunge. I could have qualified for a Breathalyzer test. But determined to master the exercise, I curtsied back and forth for a few minutes.

"How was that?" I asked.

"You look like an epileptic fish. Now, let's see if you can get a little bit more into the movement." He demonstrated the exercise. "See? Watch how I contract my abs and lower myself. Boom. Like that."

I lowered my knee halfway to the ground and then collapsed to the floor.

"Okay, that's better. We'll try some weighted squats and work in some jumps with them. See how that goes."

He handed me a twenty-pound dumbbell. I was supposed to hold it like a goblet while, for twelve repetitions, squatting as low as my butt could reach without falling. Then I was to do ten squat jumps. I'd repeat the protocol three times.

"This is going to burn. It won't be that long until your legs and your core feel like somebody has taken a blowtorch to them or feel like a dog's ass on a hot summer day," he said. "You've got to fight through it. Pain is a state of mind. At the end of the day, when I'm on my bike and my lungs feel like they're going to explode, I don't let the pain stop me. This is well within your strength. You just have to want to do it. Don't lollygag."

Darko's words resembled the Anorexia God's advice to welcome the physical discomfort necessary for achieving a greater goal.

"I don't think I can do that many squats, Darko."

"Don't even fucking get me started on not being able to do it. Just do them. I know you can do it. At the end of the day, if you say you can't do it, you won't do it. It's all fucking mental. It's all up here." Darko pointed to his temple and continued explaining the mental game. "If you've eaten three-quarters as much as you say you have, there's no reason you shouldn't be able to do this. I have an eighty-five-year-old client who can squat more weight than this. She can also do more than double the reps. So you can absolutely do this."

"I don't know, Darko."

"You're going to do it. I have nowhere to be. If we have to stay here for three days, we'll stay."

With my legs trembling, I moved the weight out in front of my chest and struggled through the twelve squats.

"See! Dude! That was great. You did it!"

The room was rotating. I crashed to the floor, resting my head and ghostly face on a padded mat.

Darko knelt down beside me. "You have to get up. The longer you lie down, the worse you're going to feel. I can absolutely promise you that."

"I can't get up. I just can't do it, Darko."

"No, if you keep moving, you'll feel better much faster."

Despite thinking Darko was wrong, I followed his advice. He was right. The nausea subsided after I stood up.

"Check out my legs," I said, aiming to sidetrack him. "Do you have anything in your teeth? You could floss them with these little sticks. I'm sure you'd like that."

"You're really a sick fuck. Walk around a bit."

"I can't do it."

Darko purchased an electrolyte drink from the vending machine. "Drink this then. Your blood sugar is really, really low. When you're working out, you need to replace the carbs that you're burning."

"I had plenty of carbs before the workout."

"Clearly not enough. You're like an underfed Chihuahua. Drink this."

I panicked. The eight-ounce bottle contained fifty calories and fourteen grams of carbohydrates from sugar.

"You could gain weight from that," the Anorexia God said. "Darko is telling you to go eat six huge meals."

"Sure, that's possible, but Darko won't let up until I drink this, and I don't want to puke on everything."

"Why the hell not? Puking means more weight loss. That's brilliant. Darko can tell you what to do all he wants, but you're in control. Suffering is strength."

"I want to feel better, so I'll drink some of it. Is that a fair compromise?"

"Fine, but don't drink more than a quarter of the thing. Thirteen calories is bad yet manageable. We'll cut it from somewhere else tomorrow and for the rest of the week."

I sipped the drink, observed the amount I had consumed, and closed the bottle when I'd reached the approximate quarter point.

"Drink more," Darko said.

"I'm full and feel much better," I lied. "Thank you for the drink. What's the next part of the workout?"

"The next part of the workout? Look at you. You probably think that you're Tinker Bell in Lebanon right now. You're done for the day."

"It's been like fifteen minutes. I'll be fine. I can do more. I'm good. Let's go."

"No, you can't. Go home, and get some food in you. I'm concerned about you. Your dad says you're not eating nearly enough."

"My dad will worry about anything. I'm sure he has some special posture to avoid hurting your back on the toilet or a stretch to keep your testicles in the right place."

"He's really anxious, but I can see that he has a point here. Someone your age who has been working out for a couple months shouldn't be on the floor and almost puking after this level of exertion. Maybe you're not adding up what you're eating correctly. All I know is that it's not enough. You can have a vegetarian hippie-dippie diet if you want to. That's fine. It doesn't mean you don't need to eat. Fuel is imperative."

"I'm eating."

I was justifying myself to Darko because I worried he'd tell my parents about my challenges. I didn't want their pressure to eat.

"You can't drive a car for hours without filling it up with gas first," Darko said while slapping his hand on a barbell.

"That's true. But the car malfunctioning doesn't mean that it's out of gas. Fuel is a necessary but insufficient component of a car working."

"Certain problems aren't that hard to detect, and this is one of them. I can tell by the way you look and the weight you've lost that you're not eating enough, and I'm worried about that. If you want to make any progress at all in the gym while you're away at school, you've got to eat more. It's a really simple equation."

"I won't give in and agree that I'm not currently eating enough, but I will increase my intake if that makes you happy, Darkman. Maybe I need to do that. It's going to be difficult because my diet is pretty piggish as it stands. I eat like a German bodybuilder."

"That's bullshit. Now, go take a shot of wheat ass or leftovers from the lawn mower or whatever that hippie shit you drink is, and have a good year at school. Just eat more, and you'll start to see progress in the gym."

"That's the plan."

"Good. Now, go home and eat, you maggot."

I left the gym and ate nothing but a few carrots for the rest of the day.

CHAPTER 6

Who's Your Daddy?

September 5, 2010

I was one day away from moving to Kingston, a quaint city about two hours east of Toronto, to start my bachelor of arts honors program at Queen's University.

"Are you ready to go? Ready to exercise that mind of yours?" Dad, who was standing outside my bedroom door, asked. "Promise me one thing: I don't want to have any grandchildren when you come home, okay? Keep it covered if you need to. Wrap the monster. Put a sock on the—"

"Oh my goodness, Sam," Mom interjected. "Do you always have to be so disgusting? You're such a pig. I am sorry you had to grow up with him as your role model. I mean, really."

"Ell, I'm just saying."

I was sitting at my desk as a spectator to a conversation about myself.

"You're always just saying, Sam."

"Like I said, I just don't want to have little grandkids running around the house. I'm serious. They're a lot of work. That's all I'm saying."

"You are such an idiot." Mom laughed. "Your father is

a moron, Jake. Do you feel bad that this is what I have to put up with?"

"You married him. He's your precious jewel," I said.

"Okay, Jake, I need to show you something," Dad said, motioning to a binder.

My father has long organized his life with binders. There are few issues he doesn't sandwich between cardboard and colored plastic. Planning a day trip to Buffalo? Binder. Buying a new phone? Binder. Getting a colonoscopy? Binder.

The expert left my room, returned, turned off the lights, and blasted "The Imperial March" over my iPod speakers. He reentered holding a black binder over his head as if he were Rafiki presenting Simba to the Pride Lands.

"Dad, is this really necessary?" I said.

"No, but I actually need to show you a ton of things. This is very important."

Both of my parents had bad habits of sending Maddie and me away with copious information. Because we couldn't ready ourselves to their satisfaction, they took over our preparation duties. Mom would have millions of instructions.

"Your scissors are in the front pocket. Now, I've packed you twenty-one toothbrushes just in case you get sick, lose one, drop one on the floor, or decide to wipe your ass with one. If your nose gets itchy, here is some special cream I got from my homeopathic guru. It's supposed to make you feel so much better. Marla and Goldy absolutely swear by him. They say he's great—solves every infection or little thing they get. You should probably see him when you get home, and maybe he could do something about the rash on your arm. Oh, I packed you a new jacket. It's a good in-between-fall-and-winter jacket. It's not too fall and not too winter. Make sure you use it. Let me just show you one more thing. I've put a pair of tweezers in between the two sweaters. They're good for ingrown hairs if you ever get them. I know you'll call me later to ask me where the tweezers are, so know that they are there."

Dad brought the binder to my desk. He flipped through papers of lease information and bills that didn't need to be printed.

"So we've got your apartment insurance here," he told me, pointing to the appropriate item. "Like I said, in case there's a hurricane or a nuclear attack, call Ceni. He'll handle it."

Dad's tone is usually urgent and reflects a self-proclaimed expertise in many fields. He is a medical doctor (human and veterinary), lawyer, botanist, aviation engineer, airline pilot, automobile mechanic, boat mechanic, property manager, electrician, and meteorologist. He loves to invent problems so he can solve them.

"You got it all?"

"Yes, I remember everything," I said.

"Let me show you one more thing," he told me, pointing at the flashlight. "Now, in case there is a power failure, this is a flashlight."

"Really? So that's what those silly-looking things are for?" I said. "I've never before seen something so crazy. Wow. Technology is nuts these days."

"Jake, I'm just saying."

Mom and Dad left my room. I didn't see them again until the next morning.

On the day I was leaving for Queen's, Dad was a moving expert. I sensed an additional level of urgency in his voice.

It was six forty-five in the morning. The moving truck was probably more than two hours away from our house, yet he was dressed and strapped into his back brace.

Despite their nagging, I was going to miss my parents. I'd been away from home for six weeks at one time, but I had never lived elsewhere.

I was at least excited that in my new location, nobody would monitor and bother me about my eating habits, which would give me more freedom to submerge myself deeper into anorexia. I was still going to be homesick. I hoped the moving truck would be late, so I could spend a few extra minutes hugging Molly, who was on the floor. She looked cuddly and cute. It was as if she could sense that suitcases indicated somebody's imminent departure. "Don't go," she may have been saying in dog-speak.

Dad exited my room and allowed me to pack a few last-minute items. The movers arrived a couple of hours later.

"All right, the movers are here," Dad announced while sprinting down the stairs.

"Holy shit, slow down, Sam," Mom said. "They still have to get to the door. I promise you they aren't going to leave."

I remember the exact time the moving truck pulled into our driveway: 8:47 a.m.

"Be careful picking up these boxes. Watch your backs," Dad instructed the movers as if they were new to lifting.

There was something odd about watching strangers haul away most of my life's contents to a new place. Home would become a destination for which I'd need to pack.

The idea of home as a vacation center had kept me awake the night before my departure. At 10:06 p.m., Maddie had knocked on my door and asked to sleep in my room. I would have normally asked her to leave or fantasize about mothering Justin Bieber's children elsewhere, but I wanted her close to me.

"Could I come in?" she asked with tears in her eyes. She sat at the foot of my bed. "It's not going to be the same without you here. I'm going to be so lonely."

"No, you won't. I'm not going that far, and I'm going to visit a lot—that is, unless I turn to a life of cocaine and LSD. Besides, Mom and Dad are here, and you are rarely home anyway. You have eight billion friends, so you won't miss me that much. You're welcome to come check out Kingston."

"That still doesn't mean things will be okay here. I'm out a lot, but you're my big brother, and I like having you here."

"I'm not going to be far away. It's not even a three-hour train ride. You're always welcome at my place."

"I'm going to come every weekend."

"Okay, that may be a bit much."

"No, I'm coming every weekend."

"Hey, you get to do some interesting stuff in school this year. I think you're reading *The Great Gatsby*, which is my favorite book. It's brilliant. I can recite most of it. Gatsby believed in the green light—"

"Like, ach. Who cares about reading? School sucks. Like, ach. Seriously, it fucking sucks."

"School doesn't suck. Enjoy your education. Embrace it."

"You're not even going to be here to help me with my homework. This is the worst. Why do you have to go? I'm going to miss you so much. We need you here. You're the leader of the house. Everyone looks up to you. You do so many things for so many people."

Hours went by, some of them in almost complete

silence. By three in the morning, my beeping stopwatch and intermittent sniffling were the only sounds left in the room.

We arrived in Kingston around ten the next morning. It was a scorching, sunny day. Moving trucks and sweating parents besieged the streets. One of those parents was huffing and puffing while sitting on an old couch in the lobby of my apartment building. He put his half-bald head into his hands and leaned over the worn-out tile.

"The elevators aren't working," he told us.

"Oh fuck," Dad said, biting his lower lip. "Your apartment is on the ninth floor."

We had to bring my stuff to the ninth floor of the building.

"You're going to get good exercise," an elderly man sitting in a walker across the couch said, laughing.

After jogging nine stories, I entered an empty unit. The entrance led into the tiny kitchen with a black-and-white checkered vinyl floor. The kitchen was run down. It had an old white fridge with stained-glass shelves and drawers. Laminate countertops that might have once had a light blue base were now dark blue with black dots. Like the silver aluminum sink, a white electric stove with four black burners was full of brown stains. Above the countertops were chipped white cabinets with large white knobs. Similarly chipped drawers lined the counters.

The kitchen led into an ovular space with a dusty glass light fixture under which a dining room table was supposed to sit. On the far wall, a sliding glass door opened to a concrete balcony with a rusty white railing. The sliding door faced an indented wall with a beam jutting out. A living area was sandwiched in between the two walls.

Beyond the entrance, kitchen, and bathroom, the rest of the space was finished with worn beige carpet and painted in white to go along with the white popcorn ceilings.

"Welcome to your new home," Dad said.

I didn't react and walked through a narrow pathway to the bathroom, which was crammed in the middle of a storage closet and my bedroom. The bathroom had small, grimy square pinkish tiles, a rusty white sink with silver taps, a rattling toilet, and a shower-bath with a peeling surface.

Without furniture, my bedroom looked like a small square. Light brown doors with large circular doorknobs enclosed a closet that couldn't have been more than three feet deep. Across the room was a small sliding window.

"What do you think?" Dad asked.

"It's nice to be here," I said tepidly. "I guess we should unpack."

My grandparents had come along to check out my new digs.

"It's homey," Nana Sheila, my paternal grandmother, said.

"It really is," Zaidy Paul, her husband, added.

"Okay, let's get at this," Dad said as movers loaded a dark gray three-seat couch into the living room.

Before the elevator started working again, I made at least ten trips up and down the stairs to collect the filled plastic boxes sitting in the lobby.

Dad was hanging framed pictures on the walls. A wall-sized image of a double-decker London bus went above the couch. The red bus was the only color in a shot of a busy London Street. On the living room wall closest to the door, he hung a plaque-mounted *Toy Story* poster.

Straw Man

The movers were putting together a round two-piece white table with metal legs that I had taken from the basement of a house that Bubby Pearl and Zaidy Jerry, my maternal grandparents, had just sold. I thought about the many dinners I'd eaten and the Hanukkah gifts I'd opened on that table and wondered whether its new location would eliminate its nostalgic value.

Mom, Bubby, and Nana began washing, unpacking, and putting away kitchen supplies.

At lunchtime, Nana and Zaidy Paul left. Bubby helped my mom make my bed and organize my clothes. Dad scrubbed the vents. While everyone else was working, Zaidy Jerry and I watched a baseball game on the new flat-screen television that rested atop a gray plastic stand. Zaidy Jerry's eyes were half open. Maddie checked her Twitter account, probably wishing she could keep up with the Kardashians.

My stomach began to hurt in the midafternoon. I hoped the process would go into the evening because I dreaded my family leaving, but by around four in the afternoon, my apartment was fully furnished and unpacked.

"Stay for dinner," I said in a hushed tone.

"No, Jake, we have to get home," Mom replied.

A lump captured my throat.

"Let me show you around," Mom said, motioning for me to get up so she could give me a tour. "There is toilet paper in the linen closet. Your forks are in the kitchen drawer. There are a bunch of extra plates under the sink. You have a citrus juicer in the cupboard. I put your shoes in the closet beside the fire extinguisher. You have chickpea salad in the fridge. Baseball hats are in the linen closet. Underwear and socks are in these plastic drawers. Don't forget that if you are looking for your Tylenol, it's in the medicine cabinet."

I wasn't internalizing anything she said, for the thought that they'd leave soon overwhelmed me.

"And that's it," she said, pointing to the made bed. "That's—"

"All right, Jake," Dad interjected. "A lot of brainpower is going to be used here."

They all walked to the entrance and put their shoes on.

As we walked down the dimly lit carpeted hallway toward the repaired elevator, they assured me that everything was going to be all right.

"You're going to do great," Dad said. "You'll kill it."

"I agree," Zaidy said. "You were meant for this."

I felt as if they recognized that a frog was jumping around the back of my throat, but they didn't mention anything about it. The frog was the elephant in the elevator.

Mom burst first.

"Please be good, and be healthy," she told me when we reached the ground floor. She sobbed. "Make sure you eat."

"Of course I will. Why wouldn't I eat?"

I was lying to comfort her. They walked out of the elevator toward the backdoor exit, which was adjacent to the emergency stairwell. I hugged them and then climbed a few steps.

"Take the elevator," Bubby said.

"No, I could use the exercise."

"Okay then."

"Goodbye," I said with my lips quivering.

I ran up one flight of stairs, and their voices disappeared with the thud of a door closing.

I must have stood alone crying in the same spot for half an hour. I was crying because I was afraid of the harm I was planning to inflict upon myself. Being serious about an endless quest to lose weight meant I'd eventually get sick. I knew that my caloric intake would get to a level low enough to jeopardize my life. If the anorexia were going to kill me, I believed I'd have died on my terms.

But the prospects of the pain in reaching those terms scared me. I was devoted to the Anorexia God but wondered about the pain that would accompany this pilgrimage.

When I returned to my apartment, I heard obscure noises coming from next door. My neighbors were enjoying each other's company.

"Harder, harder, harder. Yes, yes, yes. Oh my God!" a high-pitched woman's voice screamed through the thin wall.

"Who's your daddy? Who's your daddy?" asked a grunting man. "Tell me."

Slap. Slap. Slap.

"You're my daddy. Yes, Jeremy. You're my daddy. Be my daddy. Yes. You're my fucking—"

"Can I try your armpit?"

That was a real question.

"You can try whatever you want to," she grunted. "I feel like I'm at the—ah. I feel like—ah. Ah, yes. Moo. Ah. Moo. Ah. Mooooo. I feel like I'm at the zoo. You are like a handsome giraffe, and I am a cute, tight little baby monkey. Moo."

"Oh yeah, I like monkeys." He coughed. "Could you make monkey noises, monkey? Do it now. Yeah. Huh. Huh. Huh."

The woman squealed in a way that not even the most intoxicated monkey has ever squealed.

"Who's your daddy?"

"You're my daddy, babe. You're my fucking daddy. You are—"

I slipped a note under their door:

> Dear Jeremy and woman playing the role (I hope) of his daughter,
>
> I am not your daddy, so I don't need to hear you keep asking me whether I am. Also, monkeys don't sound like that.
>
> Yours truly,
>
> A neighbor

I chuckled at my note yet quickly grounded myself in my new reality. Besides the neighbors' exotic sound effects, I was alone, free to practice anorexia and ruin my body without interruption. I wondered whether I'd live past April. The momentary laughter couldn't take my mind away from the danger I was about to face. The pain that was coming scared me.

Desperate to leave the suffocating apartment, I ventured onto campus, where orientation activities were afoot. They called the orientation "frosh week." I hadn't signed up for any frosh-week activities, as I didn't think that party lifestyle was for me.

I reached the so-called student ghetto, a small area of narrow streets with dilapidated housing. At least one feature of each house was crooked. The grass was a pale shade of green I'd never seen before. Some students might have watered their lawns with booze.

I was walking through a community of sameness.

Students and red Solo cups filled almost every one of the weirdly colored lawns. They were all playing songs by the Black Eyed Peas. The uniform was plaid button-down shirts for men and skin-tight black skirts for women. They talked in shouts. Every property had a fold-up table on which students played drinking games.

"Nice shirt, faggot!" a uniformed guy yelled at me from an open window in his house. "Fucking faggot!"

Before I could respond, a beer bottle fell from a high-rise, missing my head by a few inches. I paused to absorb how close the glass had been to knocking me out.

"Nice shirt, faggot!" the same guy yelled at me again.

I ignored the antagonism. The scene was too much of a blur for me to process his heckles. I found a bench on the campus's main street, where I watched a collection of first-year students create a human circle in which they introduced themselves.

"Hi. My name is Teresa," one student said. "I am soooo excited for my university experience, but I'm really nervous because I hear that exams require you to retain a lot of information. Even though I'm good at that, I'm nervous, so I've started reading ahead this week. All summer, I practiced reading and memorizing content. What else is there about me? I play the oboe, like a tall glass of water before bed, am a huge fan of KC and the Sunshine Band, and love Miss Vickie's sea salt and vinegar chips. My mom sent me three boxes of chips, and I store them underneath my bed. Oh, and I collect pocket-sized action figures."

She removed a pair of Pokémon action figures from a fanny pack she was wearing around her waist. I thought that by the third day of orientation week, this woman was going to be using Pikachu as a penetrative toy in bihourly orgies. She had that band-camp vibe.

The group soon left, and the campus erupted.

"Our team is dynamite. Boom, boom, we're gonna win

tonight. Louder! Louder! We're gonna win tonight!" a group of first-years were chanting.

"Ooolay, olay, olay, olay, ooolay, ooolay. Flip cup!" another crew sang.

A muscular, pale frosh in a tank top shouted, "Yeeeeah, buddy boy! Fuck the po-lice. Fuck the po-lice, yo. Fuck the fucking pigs. You ma ni—"

"Fight. Fight. Fight. Fight."

"Frosh week. Woo!"

"Tits."

"Let's go to Ale House."

"Yeeeeah."

"Tits."

"Let's fuck shit up."

Amid the sounds of freedom, a woman tapped me on the shoulder. *Ah, will I finally have somebody with whom to talk?*

"Do you know where Princess Street is?"

I pointed toward the direction in question, and she continued waddling toward her destination. My mind reimmersed itself in the hypnotic noises.

On a lawn covered with red Solo cups, a herd of drunks was shouting song lyrics.

"Woo! I love this song so much."

I couldn't escape the party to which nobody invited me. As everything was happening around me, I aimlessly walked through the crowded streets, hoping that somebody—anybody—would need directions again. I'd never hated an artist as much as I did the Black Eyed Peas that night.

"I am your father," the Anorexia God said. "You won't feel this loneliness for much longer. Follow me to clarity. Everything's going to be okay, Jake. Our future together is very encouraging."

"I believe you, but frosh week is too much for me. I need a break before this all gets going."

The screaming, screeching, and banging were unavoidable. While I knew where I was, I was lost. I ran back to my apartment and packed a small duffel bag. Since the official beginning of the school year was a week away, I didn't need to be in Kingston. I booked the next available train to Toronto, where I stayed until the first day of classes.

CHAPTER 7

The Queen's Debating Union

My courses were annoyingly introductory and definitional.

"Can someone name one example of a politician?" a professor asked.

Was our high school education system that bad? One professor dedicated two classes to reviewing the syllabus, previewing the material that anybody could have read.

However, joining the Queen's Debating Union (QDU), the first on-campus group to which I belonged, busied my schedule. I had debated in high school and defeated inexperienced opponents, but I'd never been successful at external competitions. I was confident that the training materials and expertise the QDU offered would facilitate my improvement and help me overcome my worst and most unpersuasive habits.

The QDU held practices on Wednesday and Thursday nights. Many of our debaters competed in tournaments in other cities almost every weekend. These tournaments were entirely student run. The hosting debating club would arrange food, hospitality, and logistics. Fellow debaters judged the rounds.

In the first semester, we debated in a style called British Parliamentary. Each debate in this format consists of four teams of two people. Fifteen minutes before a round, the chief adjudicator of the tournament announces a motion and assigns sides to all of the participants. Your beliefs do not matter, as you have to make a seven-minute speech defending a predetermined position. When the round ends, the judge or judging panel ranks the teams from first to fourth and evaluates the eight debaters' performances.

Friday night consisted of two debates, while Saturday had three. Rounds took place on campus and rarely had spectators. The top eight teams then qualified for the semifinals on Sunday. Nonqualifying debaters, usually at least a hundred people, watched those rounds.

My first tournament was the Central Canadian Novice Championship at McGill University in Montreal, a city three hours from Kingston. Only new debaters were eligible to compete in the tournament.

I met the members of the van I'd travel in outside the main building on campus. Petrified that I would embarrass myself in the presence of this foreign social group, I buried my anxiety in lewd humor.

"Have you heard of vajazzling?" I said a few minutes into the drive. "It's all the rage."

"No, what's vajazzling?" Will, who was driving what I called the Vanguard, responded.

"I think I've heard of it," Dagmara answered. "It's been in some girlie magazines recently."

"Well," I said, "it starts with a Brazilian wax. Then they decorate the woman's area with Swarovski crystals. You could get any design you want. If I were a woman and wanted a beautiful Will face on my pubic zone, I'm sure they could do that. Crystalized Will. Or I'd go all red, so you wouldn't know when I was on my period."

"That's awesome," Stuart bellowed.

Stuart, a self-described Conservative Party hack who referred to his party leader as Mr. Harper, was my debating partner that weekend. He was both terrifying and comical, as his booming, deep voice conveyed imminent danger, yet his tone's seriousness often didn't reflect the content he was delivering. He could have turned *Goodnight Moon* into a harrowing drama. I learned that his intense exterior didn't match his warmth.

Stuart was a selfless partner. He was never demanding. When we lost, he wrote down tips on how to improve instead of blaming others. He never viewed a round's results as cosmically significant, eliminating the possibility of a tantrum.

However, during debates, Stuart was a controlled nutcase. Before a speech, he'd stand with his back to the judge, jump into a 180-degree turn, and roar the customary "Thank you very much" while slamming his fists on the desk. One judge recommended that Stuart try to speak to a room with ten people in it rather than pretending he was leading a political rally. After a debate concerning whether the PGA should ban Tiger Woods from pro golf, a judge commented that he had never seen anybody get as worked up about golf as did Stuart.

Although we didn't qualify for the quarterfinals, I loved debating with Stuart. He made me laugh and helped take away the initial panic. The Novice Championship weekend was the most enjoyable few days I'd experienced in many years. Despite missing my competitive goal, I was ecstatic about the prospects for my social future.

On the Saturday night, I went to a bar with my new friends. I even chastised Stuart for choosing math homework over our nonsense. I talked to real live drunks. I danced to Black Eyed Peas music. I got lost on the streets of downtown

Montreal, singing the theme song to *Arthur*, until we reached our hotel at three forty-five in the morning.

Nirvana came from pretending to plunge testicles (a tea bag) in a cup and watching Jimmy throw up into a Madonna T-shirt. Misbehavior opened my mind to treatment I'd never considered: laughter with friends.

I credited this breakthrough to the Anorexia God rather than my extroversion.

"Don't for one second think you've done this. Do you think people want to be with you and like you because of some shock humor? Please. Don't be naive," the Anorexia God said. "This is my doing."

I chewed on that. Of course no one would want to be with me or like me. Why would they? I was awkward, unattractive, and fat. But the Anorexia God was going to help me change that. "You're right," I said. "I believe in you. I serve you."

"When was the last time you ate?" the Anorexia God said.

"I had two baby carrots today and one half of a cucumber, which I measured with a ruler, yesterday, but other than that, I haven't eaten in three days. I've had water and some tea. That's it. I haven't really eaten in three days. Before this semi-fast, I had small bowls of lentils and quinoa each day."

"Good man, Jake. Keep at it."

"I'm willing to do the work. I'm submitting to you."

"Look at what's happening here, Jake. We've put down a foundation. You stayed out late. You were youthful tonight."

The anorexia was working as if it were a drug that needed time to kick in. It hadn't thrived until the tournament, but as soon as I absorbed its chemicals, I thought the euphoria would be limitless.

"Keep up with these little three-day fasts," the Anorexia God said.

"Damn right. I'm happy. I'm actually happy. When was the last time I could have said that?"

"I couldn't even tell you."

"I love you."

Kendall tiptoed into the room, trying not to wake Stuart.

"Did you see your ex?" Jimmy said.

"Yeah, man," Kendall said.

"Did you do her?"

"Yeah, man, I did. I—"

"Yeeeeah, buddy. Well done," Jimmy said, prompting Stuart to roll over in the bed that he and I were sharing thanks to the Union's limited accommodations budget. "Attaboy."

Jimmy puked into an ice bucket that he ripped from the dresser.

"Was she that bad?" Kendall chuckled.

"Man, debating tomorrow is not going to be fun at all, dude," Jimmy said, lifting his head from the stainless steel. "It's gonna be a major bi—" He puked again. "Dude, when did I have fries? I don't remember that. Oh, wait. Never mind. I forgot I ate them at that little Italian joint on that street."

"Since when did fries have hair on them?" I said.

"Dude. Duuude. She wasn't that hairy, dude. Bro, that's fucked up."

"I never implied that."

"But she was fucking epic, man."

"With that, I'm going to bed, fellows," I said.

At five thirty in the morning, I closed my eyes on a darkness that I didn't want to disappear.

"Good night," the Anorexia God said. "Great night."

CHAPTER 8

Beating Myself

My first year in the Queen's Debating Union was competitively mediocre. I couldn't consistently perform well. However, most tournaments had novice finals or championship rounds for first-year debaters. I won two of those.

My first victory was with Katherine Fu, whom I called by her Chinese name, Fu Zhong Yuan. Her ideas were usually brilliant, yet she lacked confidence. After almost every round, she thought we'd lost. The other team could have thrown up on the dais and rubbed their vomit in the judges' faces, and Katherine would have told herself that the panel might have found the puke compelling. Katherine always complimented my speeches, even the idiotic ones.

I still recall our dreadful novice final at the Father Roger Guindon Cup. We were debating in an auditorium of more than a hundred hungover students. I entered the room and walked down four stadium steps, running my fingers over the gray acoustic tiles. Two debaters in the audience were arguing about affirmative action.

"I think you should get into a program on merit alone," a guy in an oversized hoodie and sweatpants said.

"And that's the fucking problem," another guy in an

oversized hoodie and sweatpants responded, waving his arms wildly. "People are often held back by their circumstances. To say they don't have merit is so fucking problematic. It's just really shitty."

I wasn't nervous. My mind fixated on not eating rather than the debate.

The motion was "This house would abolish life sentences without parole." We were the second opposition. The first proposition team, which was supposed to debate the motion, were so hungover that they either didn't understand English (their first language) or were still drunk. Their first speaker opened the round with "We define this debate as 'This house would institute a universal death penalty without appeals because one bullet is cheap.'" His team automatically lost, but he forced participants to deviate from the topic for which they'd prepared. Whereas Katherine made serious arguments, I devoted six and a half of my allotted seven minutes to making fun of this clown.

The audience laughed with me.

"Look at that," the Anorexia God said as I paused to let the audience settle from their laughter. "You're making people laugh. We are doing this."

Katherine and I won the championship. We received maple syrup as an award because they didn't have real trophies (maple syrup is not a standard Canadian award or trophy replacement).

The Anorexia God's tone changed after our victory. He disrupted my internal celebration.

"Katherine would have won without you," he said.

"Yeah, I know. That's true."

"So why are you happy?"

"I'm happy I had a part in her winning. She deserved it."

"Bullshit. You had no part in her winning. Don't be smug. You're saying that you're the best all of a sudden?"

"We were a team."

"Which she carried."

"You're right."

I plodded back to the car, in which I pretended to sleep, not wanting to show people my sadness in the aftermath of triumph.

My second victory was with Adam Kovacs-Litman, my fellow scalawag in the QDU. A couple of hours before the tournament's first round, I said to him, "I'll blow you if we break to quarters." I didn't realize that Jerome, the club's photographer, or Peeping Tom, was videoing me from the corner of the room. If I ever run for public office, I'll have to pay Jerome for the footage. Perhaps writing about it in this book is getting ahead of the story. Thankfully, Adam and I missed the quarters by a few spots.

Like my success with Katherine, my title with Adam didn't make me feel accomplished. My unrelenting depression subdued the enjoyment I should have garnered from the achievement.

"Debating with you was a lot of fun, Jake," Adam said. "I learned a lot. I didn't know that oral circumcision was legal in New York."

The Anorexia God demanded I ignore a compliment that nobody could have meant.

"He's saying all of that to be nice."

"Maybe he actually likes debating with me."

"Why would he like that?"

"Because I'm a good person."

"You're not a good person."

"Yeah, you're right."

When I returned to my apartment that night, I picked up a framed picture of myself as a toddler and smashed it against the kitchen counter. I wished I'd never been born.

Partnering with Amelia McLeod was my most painful debating experience. She was an excellent partner—compassionate and talented—but I hated myself for wrecking our chances of competitive success. We debated at a tournament in Halifax, a city on the eastern coast of Canada and a three-hour flight from Toronto.

I followed every intelligent thing Amelia uttered with something about which even my ten-year-old self would have said, "Dude, that's really dumb." Not eating anything other than a few pickles and peppers for three days until the tournament didn't help me think clearly and argue cogently.

Unlike Katherine and Adam, Amelia was an experienced debater and was 77.84 million times better than I was. She claimed she enjoyed debating with me, yet I knew we were partners because nobody else had wanted to travel to Halifax that weekend.

"You failed her," the Anorexia God said. "She came all this way to debate, and you embarrassed Amelia and yourself."

"I've been following your advice and not eating. How could this happen?"

"Yes, you need to keep doing that."

"Why? It's not working."

"You'd have done even worse had you eaten more. Trust me."

"I do trust you."

"Good, because I'm the one real friend you have."

"I love you."

"I love you too."

I couldn't watch the semifinals. Those debaters demonstrated the extent of my weak performance, magnifying the self-doubt simmering in my mind. What would Amelia think of me after my failure? Would she laugh at me with her friends? Would she be miserable for the rest of the week because I ruined her weekend?

"You weren't bad at all," she told me. "You were a great partner. Thank you."

I didn't believe her. My niche, the sport at which I thought I was decent, once again left me sitting alone in my dark apartment and contemplating if my life had any value.

CHAPTER 9

Home Sick

I was nervous about returning home for Canadian Thanksgiving. In the month that had elapsed since I had last seen my family, I'd lost another twelve pounds. I was proud of that accomplishment and would have been thrilled if my peers recognized the change. However, I was afraid of upsetting my parents.

I alternated between wanting the train ride home to Toronto to pass and hoping it would drag on to give me extra time to float in the freedom of unfettered anorexia. Two buff male students were sitting across the aisle from me and were recapping the previous night's party scene.

"She was kind of crazy," one of the guys said. "Like level-seven crazy, man."

"How so?" the other replied.

"For one, she had a tongue piercing. That's kind of freaky. And then she came to my place and wouldn't fucking put out."

"Oh, that's such a bitch move. I mean, if you aren't interested, that's cool. Then don't go to a guy's place. Don't accept his invitation. No is an option. Why did she even come over?"

"I asked her if she wanted to watch a movie."

"Fuck, dude, she should be smart enough to know that no guy who meets a chick at a club is looking to watch a movie that late at night. And it was Stages, of all places. That's not where you go to find someone to hang out and watch a movie with."

"I know. Fucking bitch. I tried to make out with her once, but she was pushing me back."

"Man, she should have at least let you do that."

"I guess bitches be fucking crazy, yo."

The same topic of conversation continued for more than an hour. I was confused. They could persuade a stranger to spend time with them. For me, inviting a person, even one I already knew, over to my apartment required every morsel of courage I had. I was happy to have the company.

As the train rolled between fields of nothing, I slouched in my seat and closed my eyes. For a few minutes, everything was black, but then my mind sketched grainy pictures of contradictory thoughts. I could see Mom and Dad hugging and screaming at my skinny body. Although the weight loss horrified them, in my daydream, they were still glad to see me.

I needed to distract myself from the possibilities that could follow the journey's end, so I scanned the train and created stories and names for all its passengers. I'd highly recommend that game.

There's Suzanne. She married her brother at a pristine wedding on her husband's ranch. That white guy over there— his name is Jamarcus, and the guy beside him is his friend Gary. They've been best friends for years and recently found out that their two fathers were in love. There's Shirley. She used to have sex before large crowds. There's Yolanda. Before becoming a karate instructor, she taste-tested Dunkaroos. Do you call them therapists? And that's Sinep. He caught his wife cheating on him with his high school Spanish teacher.

The game sidetracked me from the immediate future before my mind revisited home. What were Mom and Dad going to say? Would they let me go back to school? Would they even notice the developments below the double-layered sweaters I wore to disguise my stick figure?

The train felt as if it were speeding and idling at the same time.

When it pulled into Union Station in the middle of the afternoon, I remained seated until everyone except for folks in wheelchairs had exited. I then took a deep breath, lifted a duffel bag full of laundry I was too lazy to do on my own, stepped onto an escalator, and walked down a dank corridor out to the street, where Mom, Dad, and Molly were waiting in the car.

I love my parents, but I was most excited to see the dog. She was wagging, crying, barking, shaking, panting, licking, and drooling on my jeans. I have yet to experience a human greeting that could rival a dog's unrestrained and instinctual joy upon reuniting with a family member. Hugging Molly and running my fingers through her curly black fur made my fears disappear for a few minutes. I was with my best friend, the pooch who spoke dog but understood human. On the drive home, the volume of Molly's breathing prevented Mom and Dad from saying much. However, as soon as we stepped into the house and I removed one of my sweaters, the nagging began.

"Jake," Mom said, "have you lost more weight?" She put down a grocery bag on a bench by the side door of the house and glanced at my figure.

"No, I haven't. I'd be surprised if I even lost a pound."

"You're looking really, really skinny."

"Well, you haven't seen me in a bit, so you could be forgetting what I looked like right before I left."

"No, I don't think so. You promised me you'd eat."

"Yes, he did," Dad said. "He promised he'd eat enough. Pretty much word for word. A deal's a deal."

"I haven't broken my promise, and I'm really not sure what you two are talking about. I haven't lost weight. Where are you getting this from?"

"Then step on a scale, and we'll see," Mom said. "Prove it."

"I'm not going to step on a scale like some circus freak. First of all, to get an accurate reading, you have to take off your clothes. I know that you two are into some weird things, but I won't give you a show, you voyeurs. Second of all, I haven't eaten lunch or dinner today because I had to rush to the train and didn't have food left in my apartment. I didn't want to waste anything. So you wouldn't get a proper weight right now."

I knew confessing I hadn't eaten that day was like telling two border guards that I was carrying four hundred grams of hash into the country.

Ignoring my protestations, Mom prepared an avocado-and-tomato sandwich for me.

"You've got to eat," she said, handing me the plate.

"I'm really not hungry right now. Put it in the fridge, and I'll eat it for breakfast tomorrow morning."

"Please just eat it."

"I will eat it tomorrow."

"No, seriously, Jake, you can't keep doing this—working out, losing weight, and not eating. It's really unhealthy. I'm not sure what's gotten into you. Are you anorexic?"

"Don't be silly. I'm not working out at school anyway."

"Then why aren't you eating? Why are you doing this to yourself?" Mom kept running her fingers through her hair.

"I'm not hungry right now. Don't overreact. I promise you everything is okay."

"I think you're anorexic. How else could I explain what I see?"

"You can believe that if you'd like to. There's nothing to explain. I'm not anorexic. I'm small-boned."

I sometimes thought bulimia would have been easier than anorexia was. I would've had to lie to my parents, but unless they'd installed cameras in or accompanied me to any bathroom I could access, they couldn't have observed my eating disorder. They couldn't have revoked puking rights. *Too bad I hate gagging and throwing up.*

"You know I'm always just looking out for your best interests, Jake," Mom said. "I'd do anything for my kids. I'd die if anything happened to you guys. I mean that."

For the first time, I felt guilty about my lifestyle. I'd caused Mom and Dad pain. I was the origin of the panicked expressions and sleepless nights. My desire for the ambiguous and elusive idea of control pulled me into a new identity that was going to eviscerate my parents and me. Allowing the anorexia to kill me would have been a murder-suicide.

Crying invisible tears, I ate the sandwich to calm Mom and Dad.

"Good man," Dad said.

"Good man? Don't listen to your parents," the Anorexia God interjected. "They're dead wrong."

"It must be nice to eat real food rather than the rabbit stuff you've been having out at school," Dad said.

"Even rabbit stuff would be too much," the Anorexia God said. "I can't believe you ate that sandwich, Jake. Are you insane? You should have just eaten a tomato."

"You need to go back to real food. Be vegetarian if you want, but you've got to eat," Dad said.

"You've got to stop eating," the Anorexia God said. "Your dad is telling you to get fat."

"Promise me that when you go back to school, you'll start eating again," Dad added.

"Promise me that when we go back to school, you'll stop eating again."

"If you're going to work out, you need to nourish yourself. You can't expect a car without fuel to drive to the cottage. That's what Darko says."

"Enough. Your dad doesn't know what the hell he's talking about. I am your father now. He means well, but has he been able to protect you from the isolation and loneliness? I know—that's totally outside of his control. He can't make people like you or deal with something you haven't really told him. But I can. I know how to help you. I have all the information. I am you. Listen to me. Follow me."

I consented to the Anorexia God's adoption.

"Now," the Anorexia God said, "you must do your best to throw your parents off. Make them think you're eating well."

Throughout the Thanksgiving long weekend, I dirtied plates and left them in the sink to mislead my parents. Twice, I made up stories about going for lunch with high school friends. I wound up sitting for a couple of hours in parking lots, waiting until plausible amounts of time had elapsed.

I described substantial meals that I never ate.

"What did you have for lunch?" Dad asked on the Sunday when I was supposed to be out with my boyhood friend Mathew Sherman.

"I started with a salad and then had brown rice pasta with a side of lentil soup as my entrée."

"Good man."

I was hiding in my own home. Each night, I slept for only a few hours. For a long time, I stared into the darkness and thought about how a million different existences would have played out. What if I'd been born into an athletic body? What if I had natural confidence and coolness? What if I had a different face? What if I liked myself?

When I was alone, my love for anorexia answered these questions, but at home, the observable destruction I was dumping on my parents fueled my self-hatred. I was ashamed that Mom and Dad were the cost of my first true source of accomplishment and control.

The next day, I went for a session with Darko.

"Jacob Two-Two," he said, wiping sweat from his face. Darko was sitting in the dingy trainer's office at the back of the gym. I leaned against the doorframe.

"Darko, I've missed you."

"Your dad says you haven't been eating."

"He's lying. He has no idea what he's talking about."

"Let's see about that. Are you ready to dance, my friend?"

He zipped up his black sweater and led me to the leg press. Darko loaded the apparatus with forty-five pounds per side. I sat in the blue leather seat, placed my feet on the individual leg-press plates, and pushed them out together.

"Square your feet, and give me twelve reps."

I felt as if my glutes were being stabbed, but I powered through the first set. We then did three sets of twelve reps on hamstring curls, quad extensions, and squat presses.

"Come with me," he said.

I followed him back to the leg press.

"Now the real fun begins," he said. "We're going to do

twelve reps on the leg press and then twelve jump squats one, two, three times a lady."

I got through another set on the leg press.

By the third jump squat, I was dizzy and light-headed. The gym's black-dotted rubber floor was levitating. I crumpled to the ground and put my head in my hands.

"I'm not sure I can do it, Darkman."

"What's the matter? What are you feeling?"

"I don't even know what year it is."

"Normally, I'd say it's just pain. It's mental. Some of it is in this case. But your face is white. I'm going to get you a Gatorade, and then you'll stay here until you feel better. Then you're going home."

"I'm not going home. We're going to do this."

"No, you are not. We are done today."

Darko pulled a Gatorade from the fridge. I took a few sips.

"I'll pay you back next time I see you," I whispered.

"Don't worry about it. Keep drinking that. Look, until you start eating again—"

"I am eating."

"No, you're not. This wouldn't have happened if—"

"It's just an off day."

"It's not. I know you're not eating. I can tell by looking at you that it's physically impossible you're eating enough. Until you start eating, we can't train. It's a waste of your time. There's no point. You can't come in empty. What good will that do? At the end of the day, you have to eat. That's what it all comes down to, my friend."

"I'm not empty."

I rubbed my fingers over my face and sighed. Darko was right, so I didn't protest too much.

"Yeah, you are. Look at you, dude. I'm worried about

you. Your parents are worried about you. You need to take care of yourself."

I didn't say anything

"Drink more," he said.

I took another sip of Gatorade, and the room stopped spinning. "I'm good now."

For almost a half hour, Darko and I talked about advances in sports analytics before I drove home.

On Monday morning, I mistakenly took off my sweater in front of Mom. I had spilled water on it, and unthinkingly, I changed with her in my room.

"Oh my goodness." She gasped. "Look at you, Jake." She scanned my bony shoulders, my jutting hips, and my stomach, which was sinking into invisibility.

"What's wrong with me?"

"You're concave. I have friends less than five feet tall who probably weigh much more than you do. You've got to start eating."

"I am eating. I swear."

"Answer me honestly. Are you anorexic?"

"No, I'm not. I've just been eating healthy. Everything's fine. I'm at a healthy mass."

"No, everything's not fine. You're definitely not at a healthy weight."

Mom clasped her hands together and exhaled. She stopped questioning me.

The evidence stood a few feet away from her. I was confident she could see the damage I was inflicting upon myself. That was the worst part about being anorexic. I readily accepted the hunger and self-hatred, but I hated turning my family into casualties of my condition.

I looked like death. We both looked like death.

CHAPTER 10

Ano-wheeling

November 2010

I thought a girlfriend could ease the loneliness that defined my early university experience. Perhaps the hunger made me thirsty. I believed that living by myself for the rest of the year wouldn't seem so daunting if I had a partner, so I devised a wheeling strategy. *Wheeling*, if you're unfamiliar with the term, is a millennial way of expressing that you're trying to attract a partner. I was convinced I had a unique trait that would distinguish me from other guys: I was anorexic. Have you not read the *Cosmo* magazine articles that call anorexics the most desirable partners? Apparently, women like men with nice hips. My hips were almost protruding through my skin, so women could have felt how nice they were. Do you like shoulders, women? Well, my shoulder bones were almost as exposed as they would have been on an x-ray screen. Women desire gaunt and emaciated men. They're into guys who have to check the wind forecast before leaving the house. I was so skinny that hugging me would have been boning.

Anorexia was my comparative advantage. Other men could produce confidence, swagger, and muscularity.

I couldn't keep up with their production, rendering unacceptable the opportunity cost of competing within their framework. I could have exuded some of those men's qualities, but I would have been less efficient than they were. I planned to tell every woman I was interested in that I was anorexic. I'd present myself as sensitive, intelligent, and a trailblazer against oppressive gender norms. Those qualities were supposed to provide me with a niche market that would offer diverse choices. I wrote a memo of steps to follow on the back of a crumpled essay that a professor had graded and returned.

> Step 1: Begin a conversation. Make sure to use at least five impressive words. Possibilities include *cognoscente, parthenogenesis, perfidiousness, sagacious, unctuous, anthropocentric, enthymeme, fugacious, hitherto, heretofore,* and *sycophantic.*
>
> Step 2: Hint that you have been having a bad first-year experience, so she asks what has been bothering you.
>
> Step 3: Bingo. She is wondering what's wrong with you. You are there. Tell her that you are anorexic, and hope she asks, "Really?"
>
> Step 4: Yeah, you really, really are. Tell her how anorexia is a tool through which you attempt to control the previously uncontrolled. You are trying to recover,

> but not eating is an addiction that you have
> been unable to overcome.
>
> Step 5: Tell her how much weight you've lost,
> and say that you are depressed and that the
> condition could become life-threatening.

I believed that women would think the narrative was compelling. It was as if I were wheeling a psychiatrist to take me on as a patient. My market analysis didn't consider that most women wouldn't want to double as therapists and girlfriends. I was shocked that my "I undermine gender norms" line was unsuccessful.

Shoshana Chitman, a fellow freshman in my Religion and Culture class, was the first woman on whom I launched Operation Ano-wheeling. She was tall and thin, had purple-dyed hair, and carried a permanent high that bordered on Willie Nelson levels. She reeked of weed and cigarettes. I first met her when she asked me to tutor her on an upcoming midterm test. She'd noticed that I participated in class, the professor seemed to enjoy my commentary, and I was ahead in the course readings. Shoshana offered to compensate me for helping her pass the midterm in a class she either slept through or skipped. I wouldn't accept her money but agreed to tutor her during the week before the midterm test.

"I haven't made any notes for the class," she said at the end of a class. "Do you think you could send me your notes?"

This is your chance, Jake. Don't screw it up.

"Of course I can send you my notes."

"Are you sure? I don't want to be too much of a burden," she said.

"No, not at all. You are not a burden whatsoever."

The truth was that I didn't make any notes in class, as I listened to and absorbed the material. However, enthralled by the prospect of guiding Shoshana toward an A+, I regurgitated my course knowledge into a notes package. I wrote fifteen mock tests, made sixty-five flashcards, and typed ten pages of text. My preparation was indulgent and extravagant. I cooked dinner, set the table, and scrubbed my apartment. My cell phone vibrated.

"Hey, I know this is super last minute, but I don't really feel like studying," Shoshana's text message read. "The exam isn't worth much—like 25 percent, I think—and I am just tired and totally not in the mood to look at this stuff. I'd rather burn, ya know? Sorry if I ruined other plans that you may have had. My bad."

I told Shoshana that her cancellation wasn't a problem.

"I was just hanging out here anyway. So it's not a big deal. It's not like I had to prepare anything," I wrote. "I could send you my notes if you'd like."

"Nah, actually, it's all right. I'll just wing it on the test. LOL. How are you doing otherwise?"

This is it. Time to wheel her with my anorexia.

"Well, I am anorexic."

Boom. Bam. Victory.

"LOL! You always have a witty line! No, really, how are you?"

"No, really, I am anorexic."

"Seriously? No, you're joshing me, aren't you? LOL!"

"Yes, seriously."

"Oh shit. Sorry if I seemed all rude and all. LOL. Shit, dude, that's rough."

I wasn't offended.

"It's okay. I know that people don't think men could be anorexic. For me, it's not really about trying to adhere to a certain standard of beauty. It's all about control. I used to be fat. When I took my shirt off, the whales would think I was one of them and ask me to join them for a swim. I became vegetarian in my senior year, naturally lost some weight, and became addicted to that feeling. I have lost like thirty pounds in the last few months. I just feel like I have control that I hitherto did not have."

Hitherto. You used hitherto *in a text message, Jake. Well done. That should show her that you are really smart. Nerdy and anorexic—you're a catch.*

"Oh shit, I am sorry to hear that, man. Get better, kk?"

"It's all right. I am trying to get over it. Some days are good, but most of the time, I just want to hide under my sheets. I guess I am defying gender norms."

She must really want me. Does a guy who defies gender norms not scream George Clooney meets Ryan Gosling?

"Yeah, that's for sure."

"I just feel lonely and sad."

"Jeez, that sucks, huh? Not good at all. Seriously."

Shoshana didn't know how to react. I'm sure the seventy million grams of marijuana she'd smoked contributed to her inability to respond meaningfully to my admissions. More likely, she was shocked that this guy she'd known for less than a month had puked out his complete mental-health assessment in a text message. What do you say to a person when he tells you he is anorexic before you even know where he's from?

Like every other woman on whom I unleashed Operation Ano-wheeling, Shoshana was uninterested. They were sympathetic, yet they didn't want to date an anorexic. A customer still has to pay for the product regardless of its discount. I was a lousy salesperson in a market devoid of clients who were looking for an anorexic.

I'm anorexic, so you should spend the rest of your life with me. We will have adorable ano babies. Think about how much money we will save on groceries that we won't buy. And if I ever rob a store or a bishop, I could fit so many things under my jacket without provoking suspicion. I would be better than Jean Valjean. They'd call me Skinny Jean. Just don't bring whipped cream into the bedroom. It has way too many calories.

I was oblivious to my strategy's futility. Most people don't want a first impression to be dark. The girls I pursued didn't need to hear that I was depressed and contemplating death. Committing to a long-term relationship would be tricky when the other person might not be around next week. Never mind that dinner dates with an anorexic would consist of one participant and one spectator.

I had the wheels of a comatose octogenarian.

"Are you sure you don't want to go over the midterm material at all?" I texted Shoshana.

"Yeah, dude, I'm sure. I'm way too high to even think about what Sigmund Marks thought about religion."

"Do you mean Karl Marx?"

"Yeah, whatever his name is. The guy with the mustache who thought religion was like some drug or shit. What was it? Weed? Ecstasy? Acid?"

"It was opium. And I think you mean Karl Marx. There's Marx, and there's Sigmund Freud. Marx had a gutty beard."

"Thanks. You're such a smarty-pants, OMG. LOL."

"No, I'm just anorexic and have lots of time to read."

That was my response. She was complimenting my intelligence, and my first instinct was to remind her that I was sick. It was like telling a woman who might have thought I was attractive that I'd once solved a severe acne problem by rubbing dog urine across my face.

"Yeah, that's so shitty, man," she wrote. "Anyway, I'm going to bed. LOL. Maybe I will see you in class if I show up again. I guess I have to be there for the test this time, ya know. But who says I will show up? LOL. What if I just don't even write it? It's worth like 10 or 25 percent or whatever."

The conversation ended. It was nine thirty, and the room was dark. I was exhausted yet awake. Silence slowed time and left me contemplating what would come next. What would eliminate the stillness? Would the apartment blink before I did?

I whipped a ceramic plate that had clumps of pasta on it against the wall. I was confused about why my plan was failing. Confused and dizzy, I crumpled to the floor in the fetal position. The apartment smelled of aged salad dressing and sautéed garlic. I pulled a cushion to my face and tried to sigh away the stress that came with optimism's retreat into the frigid reality that I was alone. The tomato sauce dripped down the wall like blood from a body being drained of life.

I looked to the sky as if to seek guidance from the Anorexia God. What would make my brain stop racing?

"Fast, Jake. You have to fast," the Anorexia God said.

I pledged not to eat for a minimum of four days. Merely water and calorie-free snacks, such as pickles, would be acceptable. As I uncurled from the fetal position, I was being reborn.

CHAPTER 11

The International Rail-Thin Association

Marin, a second-year religious studies student I tutored, invited me to what he called a "fucking rad-ass party" on Friday night. I knew a few people who were going to be there, but I wasn't close with any of them. They were mostly stoners who rarely showed up to class—or, as I called them, arts students. I decided to attend the outing, shunning my nerves because leaving early was an option.

Marin was short and chubby. He usually covered the top of his blond mullet with a Boston Red Sox baseball cap.

"The party is called for nine thirty. Dude, it's gonna be rad," Marin texted me. "Be there."

That night, I put on my favorite plaid shirt, my ironed Levi's jeans, and my nicest black fake-leather ankle-high boots. I shaved my face, plucked my eyebrows, brushed my teeth twice, combed my hair, applied deodorant, recombed my hair, and masked a pimple on my face with cover-up, which I'd yelled at Mom for leaving me. I smelled my armpits at least thirty-six times before leaving my apartment.

I was hyperventilating, terrified at the possibility of social failure. Was my breath okay? Did I have BO? Had my unibrow grown back in the thirty minutes since I'd plucked it? Was my nose running? It was, wasn't it?

Around seven o'clock, I went to the liquor store to pick up a bottle of wine. (Note: I am now cultured and know not to bring gifts to university house parties.)

"Excuse me," I said, motioning to a sales associate. "I'm looking for a nice bottle of wine in the price range of about eighty-five to a hundred dollars. Could you help me?"

"What types of wine does the person like?" the sales associate asked.

"I don't know. I want something impressive. You could pick something you'd drink or would be impressed by."

She pointed out a bottle of red wine with a fancy-sounding Italian name I couldn't pronounce. I had the cashier enclose the wine in a gift bag and then went to a nearby drugstore to purchase a thank-you card.

When I finished my pre-party shopping, I walked to a park a few hundred meters from Marin's house. I sat there in the chilly autumn air for just more than two hours, until it was exactly 9:28 p.m.

Intoxicated students walked through the park, carrying bags of alcohol and wondering aloud how long the line-ups at the local clubs would be.

"Are you sure you want to do this?" the Anorexia God asked. "Be very careful."

"No, I'm not sure at all. Should I go?"

"You should go. It'll be a great test of what we've done together. You've had one meal per day for the last week, so I think you're getting close to the point of being a desirable human being. You may even be there already. We'll see."

"Okay, let's do this."

I stood up from the bench.

At 9:30 p.m., I knocked on Marin's front door and was surprised that I was the first person to arrive.

He came to the door topless and in boxer shorts, through

which the outline of his penis was visible. His gut spilled over the waistband.

"Where is everybody?" I asked.

"It's very early, man. Very early," Marin drawled. "They'll be here, dude. It's gonna be so rad."

"Hmm, people aren't punctual, I guess. I got you this." Reluctantly, I presented the gift to a confused-looking Marin.

"Rad. You didn't have to do that. It's not that kind of party, dude. Thank you, though." He tilted his head to the right and accepted the wine before putting it down in a corner by the door.

"You invited me. That's the protocol when you get invited to events. My family has been doing that forever."

"Rad. That's cool, man. Family is what it's all about, right? Come on in."

His house was filthy. The hundred-year-old carpet was filled with obscure crumbs, and the sofa had been humped on before the invention of cars. On the south wall hung a partially torn poster of porn star Sasha Grey in professional attire—a nurse's uniform—to which somebody had added a handwritten caption: "God Bless Bush." I wanted to ask Marin whether he had a vacuum or rubber gloves I could use, but the only rubber I could find was underneath the cushion on which I was sitting.

He left briefly to change into blue jeans, a T-shirt with a large eyeball on it, and his Red Sox cap.

"So, dude," Marin said, adjusting his cap, "are you actually anorexic, yo?"

"How did you know? Did somebody tell you?"

"It's cool, dude. Shoshana from class told me about it," he said.

He was referring to Shoshana Chitman. The two of them were close friends.

"She's a major fox, man," Marin said. "She heard it from someone. Ya know how them women be. Am I right? Bitches gonna be bitches. They gonna bitch, yo. They'll run their mouths."

He leaned over a glass table covered in weed and pretzels to take a hit from his bong. The bubbling noise lasted for about thirty seconds. Marin blew a puff of smoke in the direction opposite where I was sitting.

He pulled from his jeans pocket a round yellow tablet with a smiley face on it. He swallowed it and then took another hit from his bong.

"Do you want some?" he said, pointing to the table.

"Nah, thanks. Yeah, man, though, I am anorexic. It's not a huge thing or anything like that."

"Rad. That's so cool. I support your movement so hard. You guys do great work. I went to one of your parades, yo. It was fucking sick. Actually epic."

"Which movement? Is there some underground ano movement singing 'We Shall Overcome' that I've never heard of? I haven't been to an anorexic march on Washington. Come to think of it, that could be fun." I paused and then began speaking in a preacher's voice. "I have a dream that one day this nation will rise up and get skinny."

"Nah, dude, I mean the gay rights movement. I'm a supporter. Big, big ups, yo. Rad."

"I support the full acceptance of LGBTQI too, but I'm heterosexual."

"I'm confused, man. So you're not anorexic?"

"No, no, I am anorexic."

"Rad, but how is that possible? That's a disease for girlie valley girls and gay guys—no offense, dude."

"None taken. Well, here I am, and I'm not wearing

stilettos. And you know homosexuality doesn't indicate certain types of gendered behavior, right?"

"Dude, right on. I didn't expect that. I learn new things every day. That's why you're my tutor, man. That's why I pay you the big bucks. Fucking rad. So rad. You're a boss."

"You don't pay me. I help you for free."

"Oh fuck, man. You should get paid."

We talked about sports for half an hour or so.

Sensing his vulnerability and bored of the conversation, I engaged my rotten habit of convincing gullible people of something ridiculous for my own amusement. I thought the laughter might make me feel better.

"Actually, I sort of lied to you," I said.

"Rad. About what, dude?" He massaged his bong.

"Promise not to tell anybody what I'm about to say, okay? This is pretty deep shit." I felt guilty for capitalizing on Marin's gullibility. At the same time, I was biting my lower lip to suppress my laughter.

"Rad, dude, I wouldn't say anything ever. I swear."

"Remember when I said there isn't an underground movement? I wasn't being honest with you."

I was exploring the boundaries of Marin's credulity. He was sweating and staring straight ahead. He wouldn't make eye contact with me.

"Rad. I fucking knew it. So you are gay, man?"

"No, I'm part of a club called the International Rail-Thin Association, or the IRA. We have a chapter here at Queen's, but the organization is based in Ireland. We are sort of like the Dead Poets Society—except we don't misinterpret Robert Frost's 'The Road Not Taken' as a call for freethinking and individuality. I hate when people do that."

"Poets Society? Jack Frost? What are you talking about, man? I'm a little lost."

"Never mind. Anyway, there are nine of us here and about fifteen thousand—it might be close to sixteen thousand—worldwide. We started in Ireland, but we're international. Our names come from all over the world. They call me Yasser Arafat-free. The president of our club's name is Herbert Hoover. He's our thirty-first president and a great man who is studying mining engineering. We also mix our allusions like I'm doing now. Please don't tell anybody about this. I could get expelled for my involvement. We used to have a really bad relationship with the prime minister of Britain, Margaret Thatcher. Things have gotten better. We're still not allowed to operate on this fascist campus. In the early eighties, the dean killed two of our members with his bare hands, which wasn't difficult to do, given how skinny they were. They're buried under the library. I'll show you where they are sometime. They aren't marked with anything. Zero markings to symbolize zero calories."

"Holy shit! Rad. Absolutely fucking rad. What do you do during meetings? I want to know. Could I come to one? I'd be silent."

"Unfortunately, we aren't accepting new members right now. Oh man, we do some crazy things during our meetings. It's the most rad. It's way too rad."

"Rad. Like what happens?"

"Well, we start with the Bulimic Death Spew Marathon, or BDSM. That's when things gets pretty real."

"What's that? It sounds intense, dude."

"Our bulimic members puke into buckets and then dump the spoils over their heads as a sign of devotion to the group. It's a team-building exercise for sure."

"Dude. That's kinda gross. But it's also kinda fucking rad." He took another hit from the bong.

"I know it's screwed up. It gets way worse. We then

discuss how we could convert people to our group and consult with our missionaries who go door-to-door. Have you ever had Jehovah's Witnesses come by your house?"

"Yeah, man, once, I think."

"Do you ever let them in?"

"Nah, fuck that. I've got too much shit to do. Get 'er done."

"Well, think about it. Are they really Jehovah's Witnesses? Do you ever ask them for the Jehovah's Witnesses license they're supposed to carry at all times? The people who knock on doors are almost always our members, but because we can't operate on campus, we pretend to be part of another religious group or to be conducting a survey on behalf of the university. Only once we are one hundred percent sure we can trust you do we reveal our true intentions and who we are."

"Rad. Dude, I had no idea. Do you do other messed-up shit? Like, is there some sort of ritual sacrifice for you guys?" Marin leaned his head back on a couch cushion.

"Lift up your shirt," I said.

"Why, dude?"

"Lift it up. Do it now."

"I need to know why. Are you trying to seduce me or something? I don't lean that way, dude. You told me you weren't gay."

"I'm not trying to seduce you. I need to make sure you're not wearing a wire."

He followed my instruction, revealing nothing but his hairy midsection.

"Good. Thank you. I can never be too careful," I said. "Look, of course we have ritual sacrifices. They're a little bit too extreme for my tastes, so I don't go to meetings on those days. They're ugly and messy—very bloody."

"So fucking rad. What do you sacrifice?"

"Our own members, of course. It's totally consensual. They sign up for it."

"Dude, you're totally fucking with me. Come on."

I scowled and looked into his glowing bloodshot eyes. "Do I look like I'm fucking with you?" I said in a hardened tone.

Marin paused before responding. "Man, you guys are hard core. Want to get high with me? That'd be so rad."

"I'm already high—we smoke the vomit of our bulimic members. In fact, that's what I was doing before I came here."

"Right on. How do you do that?"

"I can't tell you, but it's so potent, man. You have no fucking idea."

"Dude. You're a badass. Like, I never knew. I always thought you were like a nerdy tutor the teachers liked. This side of you is so rad. Holy shit. So rad."

"Please don't tell anybody about this. Check this out." I removed a red elastic band, which once had held broccoli together, from my wrist and handed it to Marin. "Wear this. It's a sign of solidarity with the International Rail-Thin Association. Don't tell a soul what it means. Got it?"

"Yeah, got it. Aw, man, I could never not eat or throw up on purpose like that, but you guys are fucking rad. I'll wear this all the time because it's fucking rad. Thanks, dude."

"I'll see what I can do about you coming to a meeting."

"That would be so rad. I wanna observe."

Six guys all dressed in blue jeans and plaid shirts walked through the door. Each of them was carrying a brown bag full of booze.

"Heeeey!" one of them yelled.

"Heeeey!" Marin replied from the couch.

"Yoooo!" another member of the plaid battalion shouted, pulling a beer can from his bag.

"Nice talking to you, Josh," Marin said to me.

People started filling the house. Within a few minutes, the place smelled like a urinal. Images of high school parties stampeded into my mind. I saw the corners of rooms where I'd sat alone.

I left before the party really started.

"See ya," Marin said, waving his red elastic at me. "Stay strong, Josh."

CHAPTER 12

Boy on the Dock

After returning to my apartment from the party, I was simmering with self-hatred. I didn't understand why I was so angry, yet I flipped over the kitchen table and smashed a CD case over my quad.

I heard my building managers banging on doors to deal with noise complaints and my neighbors taking each other to the zoo again. "Ah, yeah. This is *March of the Penguins*," she moaned.

I imagined Morgan Freeman sitting on a rocking chair across from the couple's bed and narrating their performance: "And every year, they embark on the nearly impossible journey to find a mate."

I plastered myself on the bed and wrapped my bones in the comforter. The sounds came from everywhere and revoked my power to be sad in tranquility. I signed on to Facebook to see whether there was anybody who could improve my mood, but it was a Friday night, and my friends were either in university or the late stages of high school. They were out enjoying life and not entombing themselves in negative emotions.

I glanced at a picture of a long-deceased hockey player that hung on my wall. His crew cut was groomed perfectly, and his expression conveyed contentment, an unspoken confirmation that life was fulfilling.

I needed to cleanse myself, so I leaped out of bed and into the shower. The scalding water cleared my infected sinuses.

"It's Kim, your building manager!" a voice some fifty feet down the hall shouted. "This is your last warning to keep it down!"

The almost pressure-free flow bounced off my head.

"Why the hell is this happening to me?" I asked the Anorexia God. "Why do I feel this way? Why do I want to die? This sensation won't go away."

He didn't respond, leaving me to search for nonexistent explanations under the hot water. Had I done something wrong at the party? Was I about to get a bad mark on the test I'd written on Wednesday? Was I having a premonition of an imminent nuclear attack on Kingston?

I stepped out of the shower and into the freezing open space. In a small frame on my black IKEA coffee table was an image of a grinning six-year-old version of me standing on the dock at our family's cottage. The sun was shining on my shirtless body, its flat stomach and boobless chest exposed for everyone to worship. My figure was impeccable; I was an Adonis who had just graduated from diapers.

I ran my hands over my breasts and felt large lumps of skin. They were droopy, pointy, and disgusting. I complained to the Anorexia God. "I have tits. Is this some sort of sick joke?"

Still, he didn't answer my grievances.

I changed into boxer shorts, sat on the sofa, and leaned forward to estimate how much flab would spill over my pelvis. The results horrified me. I believed that someone could have fit all the contents of a medium-sized purse into the repulsive pouch.

"What is happening to me? I'm following your diet. I'm doing everything you want me to do. This is a failure."

I pressed my chins against my collarbone. There were way too many of them—at least seven, I counted. I had the face not of a devoted anorexic but a morbidly obese compulsive beer drinker.

"What an unacceptable collection of chins," I said to the Anorexia God.

The boy in the photograph smiled at me, ridiculing my corpulence with his flawless figure. He was happy—too happy in his fake Oakley sunglasses. The lake was too passive, the sky too bright, and the boat too still.

I held the picture frame under my chin and cried to the Anorexia God.

"I want it back. I need to look like that. Please. What do I do? I need your help."

The one reply was the moaning of the woman next door, the reverberations of her weird pleasure heckling my metastasizing mental malady. "Ah, you're my pretty penguin buddy" was the soundtrack of my pain. The strange sexual shrieks, which should have been humorous, chased me. I shook as the thuds, screeches, and guffaws engulfed my apartment, preventing my lips from moving.

I slipped a shoe on my sockless right foot and dropped the picture frame on the carpet. The boy's smile expanded. I stomped on the picture frame until the shattered glass shredded the photo paper into pieces. The sole recognizable fragment displayed my face from the nose down. That stupid grin was still there, like a monster the action hero thinks is dead but then reappears and breathes more fire. Needing to complete the project, I ripped the scrap and threw it over the balcony.

I kicked off my shoe and stumbled to bed instead of cleaning up the broken glass. The sheets kept me warm yet suffocated the skinny corpse that I deemed fat. I covered myself with eight additional blankets and four sweaters. All my apparel was oversized—or, as I would say, anorexic clothing resembles hip-hop fashion.

"You did well at Marin's party tonight, Jake," the Anorexia God said.

"I did well?"

"Yeah, that's a positive. Be pleased about that. The IRA? That was funny stuff."

"How can I be pleased when I feel like this—with everything hurting?"

"Easy answer. What did you eat two days ago?"

"Nothing. I've been good."

"No, you ate something. What was it?"

"Oh, right. I had a half slice of cheeseless pizza."

"Bingo, my friend. That's why you feel this way. Food depresses you. It takes away the control you need."

I remembered that restricting food was the only way I knew how to gain control. Keeping my body in a caloric deficit would allow me to lose weight. The Anorexia God's advice made sense to me. Eating that half slice of cheeseless pizza meant I'd lost control. I'd surrendered to hunger, a sign of weakness.

"I have to go home soon. The holidays are coming up. I'm going to have to eat with my parents around."

"Find a way out of it. Do whatever you need to do. Be intelligent and cunning. You can do this."

I took a deep breath that allowed me to process the Anorexia God's promise. The solution was in suppression.

It was in my capacity to control the sizes of those foul parts that teemed with fat and again resemble the unblemished kid in the photograph. That was hope. That was freedom. That was beauty.

I pressed play on TLC's *I Didn't Know I Was Pregnant*. While my soaked eyes focused on the little computer screen, my imagination sprinted toward elusive ambitions.

CHAPTER 13

Anonymous

After three days of eating just cucumbers and pickles, I was exhausted and dizzy. But I diverted my focus from the discomfort. I wrote a short story about an anorexic man and his best friend and called it "Harold and Kumar Run from White Castle." You're all fortunate that I deleted the document fifteen minutes after I composed it.

I lay back in my bed and chewed a four-color pen until all its tubes exploded on my tongue. My mouth was colorful for the rest of the day. I researched the calories in ink to ensure I hadn't deviated from my fast.

Once I found that I was in the clear, I watched a marathon of *Hoarders* because I knew that it could help suppress my appetite. The *My Strange Addiction* episode in which a widow eats her husband's ashes would have been optimal, yet that program was a couple of months away from its series premiere.

Beyond attending my classes, I remained in my apartment for the entire week, skipping debating meetings and a lecture. It was the first time I'd felt physically sick from the anorexia. My ailments, however, didn't dissuade me from intensifying my eating disorder. I convinced myself it would increase my popularity, thereby making me feel less awkward. The cool people probably never worried how their hands dangled or whether a hair was in the wrong place. They didn't assess the potential for catastrophes to follow participation in conversations. I didn't think weight itself was a factor that would qualify me to be part of that elite group, only that the capacity to determine my appearance would grant me the confidence necessary to appear worthy of inclusion. Corporeal control, I thought, was the sole way to reach that level. Perhaps Shoshana wouldn't have canceled our study session had I been more appealing.

Food disgusted me. It was my enemy, a wicked force determined to preserve my misery and exploit my weaknesses. I enjoyed the hunger pains, for they signified success. They were the most basic illustrations of conquest—my anorexic battle scars.

"When will my ano-wheeling strategy work?" I asked.

"Be patient. You aren't there yet. You still weigh more than one hundred forty pounds, so you have a while to go."

"When can I start being comfortable with my weight?"

"Well, you'll never be fully comfortable. Think of yourself as if you were a corporation. You're always going to look for more ways to increase your profit margins."

"Sure, though corporations do set targets."

"Let's not set a target. You already had a breakthrough at the novice tournament. Keep dropping those pounds, and your ano-wheeling will begin working as well."

"You're absolutely correct."

I chugged five large glassfuls of water, which was supposed to facilitate weight loss, I'd read. The science behind the strategy was too complex for my unscientific mind to understand, but I trusted it without reservation. I couldn't gain weight by drinking water, so aside from needing to use the bathroom every ten minutes, my approach didn't have any disadvantages.

As I was finishing my last glass of water, my friend Pam sent me a text message to invite me to a study group.

"Should I go?"

"Do you have adequate energy to be interesting or not be a drag on the friends who are going to be there?" the Anorexia God said.

"No, I'd probably be really quiet and boring."

"Then you shouldn't go."

"What if I eat something small?"

"That would be really foolish. It would be worse than going on your completely empty stomach. You don't take anything seriously. That much is clear."

"I need to be better."

I believed that the Anorexia God was correct. Socializing with those I wanted to get close to was valuable if I could benefit from the interactions. That Pam was becoming one of my best friends at Queen's heightened the importance of every interaction. We'd studied together before, but I was nervous that she would recognize the uselessness I saw in myself.

"I'm sorry, Pam," I texted. "I'm not feeling great tonight."

I drank the remaining few drops of water and slept away the last eleven hours of the fast.

The next day, I followed my conventional meal-and-a-half diet. Breakfast consisted of an apple and one half of a bagel very lightly covered with tahini. Dinner was one quarter of a cup of lentils and four carrots. I measured every ingredient. A single lentil more or a tiny overflow of tahini on the spoon would have been unacceptable. My goal was to lose weight while eating enough to survive. Any plateau meant I would have to adjust the diet to maintain the stable decline.

I would exude sympathy and be the kind of person someone would want to take a picture with to post on Instagram:

> This is my anorexic friend Jacob. I love him.
> #NoFoodPorn #Anorexia2010 #CutestAno

Being my acquaintance would offer a person the opportunity to bolster his or her image, to say, "Hey, I'm friends with that awesome anorexic guy." Social media credibility wouldn't require going to developing countries to build houses and schools that somebody would throw down before the next group arrived.

I booked an appointment with my family physician, Dr. Silver, for he could provide me with a valuable social tool: verification that I was dying.

CHAPTER 14

Silver-Medal Diagnosis

My posture had never been as upright and regal as it was when I entered Dr. Silver's pristine office. Dr. Silver was my family practitioner in Toronto. I was visiting home for the weekend and went for a checkup at my mom's request.

Although she'd brought up the idea, I was happy to see Dr. Silver. I felt a sense of zeal and accomplishment as the appointment's script, which I had written many times over, unfolded in my imagination. The doctor's words would massage my self-perception, transporting me from obscurity to importance. I was excited to hear an official confirmation of my anorexia nervosa. It would be a badge of suffering that would permit me to stand tall.

My dreams of the diagnosis were colorful and rich with detail. I dreamed of sitting atop a towering blue float with two green dragons on each side of its round front; it was the central figure in a downtown parade. Marching bands that played a repertoire of cheerful tunes; hundreds of psychologists who, for some reason, wore stethoscopes around their necks; and hordes of vomiting bulimics and bony anorexics surrounded my opulent platform.

I tapped my right foot underneath the chair.

"Next," the long-haired brunette woman behind the desk said.

I approached the glass-enclosed counter, which housed two secretaries—both women—and a couple of flat-screen computers. "Hi. I'm Jacob Roth. I'm here to see Dr. Silver at eleven o'clock."

"Do you have your health card with you?"

I handed her the opaque plastic, which featured a barely recognizable shot of my once chubby face. She scanned it before inquiring about whether my address or phone number had changed since I'd last frequented the office.

"Thank you, Jacob. You can have a seat. Dr. Silver will be with you shortly."

The waiting room's quietness fed my self-ascribed superstar-status delusion; it was all clear for my visit. A thin middle-aged blonde woman whose profile didn't move from her cell phone and a hairless elderly gentleman were awaiting care. In plastic black chairs with circular holes, we all sat at different ends of the narrow beige-tiled seating area. Surprisingly, recent magazines sat on a creamy wooden desk off of which the strong late-morning sun refracted.

A shirtless six-packed man posed on the front page of a health magazine, reminding me that I shouldn't have eaten a small bowl of oatmeal that morning. If I wanted such a chiseled core, I needed to further restrict my already minuscule appetite. The cover model, I concluded, must have been invincible, successful, and well liked: the ideal man. His appearance nullified any considerations of his personality. He had the power to spoil my anorexia parade with his hot presence. Sure, I had lost a lot of weight since April, yet he was my superficial superior for whom my dreamy entourage would leave me; the marching bands would play for him instead. The high on which I'd entered the office became a depressive trough.

I experienced these wavelike mood swings frequently, so this nosedive wasn't alarming. It had a typical trivial cause: an innocuous photo of a stranger was an ample origin of grief. Happiness or any positive emotion I might have had was brittle.

"Jacob Roth," the nurse called in her motherly British accent. "Come with me, please."

I rose from the chair and followed her through an open door, past a medical equipment station, and into a free room where I'd hear identity-transforming words. I was ready for the doctor to meet my devil.

"Dr. Silver will be with you shortly."

Lying on the paper-covered table, I hoped the doctor's evaluation would match my grand expectations. Venetian blinds allowed in some sun, which warmed my chilly skeleton. Black-framed pictures of zebras roaming grass fields, Dr. Silver's framed degrees, and a plaque-mounted poster of the female reproductive system lined the creamy white walls. The floor was made of mild green sheet vinyl. A list of the day's patients, along with their ailments, glistened on the massive Apple desktop that stood atop the mahogany desk.

"Hello, Jacob," Dr. Silver said, lowering himself into a black mesh chair.

He wore gray dress pants and a white button-down shirt with three buttons open to reveal a healthy patch of chest hair. Dr. Silver spoke in a concise yet respectful matter-of-fact tone. Service over chattiness defined his practice. I was pleased he had a hint of excess midriff fat, a discovery that reassured me of my physical supremacy.

"How are you?" he asked.

"Not bad," I said. I regretted using that pleasantry. He hadn't asked me how I wasn't feeling; he'd asked me how I was. That lapse in idiosyncratic precision irked me, as it represented a poor start to what was supposed to be a flawless meeting.

"What brings you here today?" he asked.

"I haven't been feeling well lately," I said. "I'm getting a lot of headaches and don't really have any energy. I'm dizzy a lot and always need to rest. It's not interfering with my schoolwork. I completed most of my reading by October, and my marks are good, but I still feel very sick."

"Now, Jacob, your mother has expressed some concern about your eating habits. Why do you think she is worried about that? I should remind you that everything you say in here is confidential."

I wasn't surprised that my doctor would bring up comments my mom had made. She couldn't get through to me, so I thought she'd seek another route to change my behavior.

"I don't know," I lied. "I really don't."

"She also told me that you've informed her about some regrets regarding your university choice. Have you considered transferring to somewhere closer, or are you set on seeing through your four years at Queen's?"

"I'm not seriously thinking about a change. Transferring would be too complicated at this point and mess up my academic timetable."

"Okay, you know, once we make decisions, sometimes we need to live with them. Dwelling on the negatives or, um, wishing that you did something differently really will not help you."

I was getting impatient because I sought that magical diagnosis. The preamble was dull.

"My school choice isn't a big concern to me," I told him. "Do I have some regrets? Sure. That's normal, I think. Everybody regrets things. It's healthy. If you don't regret anything, then you are arrogant and will never learn from your mistakes. You'd keep pissing in your pants. But my regrets aren't to the point that I obsess over them or they change my behavior. It's not a huge deal."

Dr. Silver typed what I was saying. "That's good to hear, Jacob. Have you made friends at school? Are you satisfied with your social life? Your mother also suspects that you are lonely."

"Yes, I have made a lot of friends in the Queen's Debating Union and through a couple of my tutorials."

"Very nice. Your mother may just be concerned. Let's face it: mothers do that sometimes. But I wanted to inquire a little more about your eating habits. When I look at you now, I am not worried about your weight. But I want to make sure you are eating enough."

I swallowed a large wad of saliva and blinked a few times. "I understand," I said feebly.

"And again, everything you say here is confidential. Do you think you're eating enough?"

I didn't pause before responding. "No."

"Why do you think that's the case?"

Ah, the moment to which I'd been so restlessly looking forward had arrived. My posture was impeccable again. The marching bands were playing warm-up scales and arpeggios in my head. The parade was set to begin. Spectators lined the street to get close to my float and lob compassion baskets at me. I was their hero.

"I don't eat enough," I said. "I know that."

"What does that mean? How many meals a day do you eat?"

"It varies too much to give you a precise or even satisfying answer to that question."

"On average perhaps?" he said.

"On good days, I'll eat like a meal and a half. I think on most days, I will eat about half a meal and maybe a small snack."

"And what would that look like? Do you have an example?"

"Sure, I'll eat a veggie dog for a meal around two o'clock in the afternoon and then a Red Delicious apple in the evening."

"Jacob, you know that is an unhealthily low amount, right?"

"Yes, I do. I get that."

"Do you not get hungry?"

"When I first started eating insufficiently, I got hungry all the time. But I've reached a stage at which my appetite is really small. I rarely get hungry anymore," I explained. "I don't need to eat that much."

"Why did you begin restricting or, um, limiting food in the first place?"

"I loved and still love the control." I never made eye contact with him.

"What do you mean by that?"

"Well, on April fourteenth of this year, my grandfather's birthday, I became a vegetarian. Soon after, I began eating really well. I quit consuming sugary drinks, as before that point, I drank a lot of soda and way too many juice boxes."

Dr. Silver continued typing.

"I was disgusting before," I said. "I stopped eating junk food. Naturally, I shed some weight. My body ceased changing because I was never terribly fat or obese. I was disappointed, Dr. Silver. I didn't like that there was a plateau, so I continued to eat healthy foods, but I just ate fewer of them. Every week, I took my eating habits to new extremes, until I reached this point at which I can't eat less than I do now—well, maybe a little less but not significantly less. The control feels amazing. Of course, I know that I'm damaging my body and my organs. I understand that this is all quite serious. But I like knowing that I have this power. I can lose as much weight as I want to. My body can look like I want it to. It's nice. It's pretty cool and maybe even addicting. Even though it's very obvious that I need to change my behavior, I love the weight loss."

Playing a celebratory refrain, the trumpeters followed my now-moving float. Thousands of admirers watched, chanting, "We're with you, Jacob." I waved and smiled at the crowd to acknowledge that I appreciated their kindness. I caught and swung above my head a padded bra and lacy G-string that an unidentified woman threw at me. Pain, I reasoned, would demonstrate my dedication to the lifestyle.

"Jacob, out of everything you just said, I'm most worried about this control that you speak of."

"Oh yes, damn freaking right you are," I wanted to say. I substituted that profane idea for a meek "Okay."

"I don't like putting labels on things unnecessarily, but there is definitely a case of disordered eating here. Again, I don't want to label it and say that it's one specific condition or another. We could treat it generally right now."

That wasn't the diagnosis of my dreams. I wanted to hear death in Dr. Silver's voice and have him tell me I was anorexic. But I could now say I had a full-blown eating disorder. It wasn't formally anorexia nervosa yet was a real medical condition.

"I wouldn't think it was right sending you back to school

completely on your own in Kingston without any sort of help. Would you feel comfortable speaking to someone there?"

"Yeah," I said.

"I know that there is an eating disorder program at the Hospital of God. At least I think that's what it's called, Jacob. I'll look it up. They do group and individual sessions. Would you be comfortable with the group arrangement?"

"Yes, absolutely."

Dr. Silver pulled up information about the Hospital of God on his computer. He scrolled down the screen until he found their contact information. "Okay, Jacob. I am going to send a referral to that hospital," Dr. Silver said while typing. "You should hopefully get a call from them pretty soon. It's more likely you'll be with an individual therapist, but there's a possibility of a group setting."

He printed a couple of pages of basic information from an eating disorder clinic's website. I was most interested in the "Characteristics of an Eating Disorder" section.

Anorexia Nervosa

-Marked weight loss due to severe restriction of food intake, often in combination with excessive exercise and/or purging

-An intense fear of gaining weight or becoming fat

-Feeling fat when obviously underweight

Excluding the purging, I checked off each item on that list. I smiled internally.

"Since the term is ending and I guess you'll soon be

writing exams, treatment will most likely kick into gear after the winter break. That doesn't mean you won't have a session or two before you come home," Dr. Silver said.

"Okay."

"I am comfortable with that situation because I don't think your circumstances are, um, urgent at this point. Still, we can't let it ever get to that point. We need to get ahead of this."

"Not urgent?" I panicked. This had to be a life-threatening crisis. Dr. Silver needed to send me to a rehabilitation center immediately, maybe even as an inpatient. A minor eating disorder was neither cool nor interesting. I decided I needed to further radicalize my lifestyle and maybe even fast enough to jeopardize my existence.

"All right, no problem," I said.

We stepped into the hallway, where I stood in front of a scale. I removed my shoes and emptied my pockets. Even a penny would have been too much extra mass. I raised myself up on the scale, which produced a 58.2-kilogram figure.

"What's that in pounds?" I wondered aloud.

"That's approximately one hundred thirty pounds."

"Thank you."

I was dissatisfied, as I wanted to fall below the arbitrary 125-pound benchmark I'd set for myself when I'd reached my goal of 135 pounds two weeks earlier.

"Again, I'm not too worried about that weight, Jacob. Don't take that to indicate that I am not worried at all. That's not the case. I don't like that you were one hundred seventy-six pounds in April. We're in mid-November, so that's almost a fifty-pound decrease in well under a year. The marked loss is concerning. We need to do something about that."

"Right, right."

"I want to take your blood pressure before you leave,

and I'm going to send you for some blood tests to make sure everything is okay internally. I don't anticipate any major problems there, Jacob."

Dr. Silver returned to his desk to click a bunch of unreadable buttons on his keyboard and then printed another sheet, which he passed to me.

"Jacob, you can take this to the blood clinic. I want to test that your iron, electrolytes, and B_{12} are all where they should be. They'll also check some other vitamin levels. I don't anticipate that we'll find anything abnormal. I want to be safe. We're also going to do an electrocardiogram to be sure your heart is functioning as it should be. Again, I'm confident that everything will come back fine. The blood lab is next door, so you should try to get this done as soon as possible."

His response disappointed me. I wanted him to tell me I was on a path to hospitalization or needed rapid intervention.

"Thank you very much, Doctor."

The nurse directed me to a room near the front of the narrow corridor. She was wearing a long lab coat and roomy beige pants. Her dark blonde hair with immobile bangs fell just above her shoulders. Except for the absence of zebra images, this area shared the previous room's features. She grabbed the cuff of the blood-pressure monitor off the wall, attached it to my arm, and fumbled with its cords before untangling them.

"This may pinch a little, but it should not really hurt," she said.

I nodded before she engaged the gadget. Its subdued noises lacked the sexiness of the medical procedures I desired. For a few minutes, I felt tight squeezes on my right arm. Then the machine relinquished its grip.

"All done," the nurse said. "Have a wonderful day."

I put on my coat and released myself into the real world. Cars with blaring horns zipped by me. Pedestrians listening to music through their headphones ignored external noises. Smokers filled their lungs. The world wasn't part of my festival. I was an insignificant eating disorder patient, obscure and irrelevant.

Two days later, Dr. Silver phoned me to relay that my vitamin D and iron levels were a smidgen too low and that I needed to take daily vitamins to correct those deficiencies. Other than that, everything was normal. I was displeased with the diagnosis. It lacked any gravitas. I vowed to make the solution to my medical problems much more intensive than vitamins. It was time to plunge deeper into an anorexic abyss and bestow some dignity upon myself.

I postponed the parade.

CHAPTER 15

Sinking Deeper

December 2010

I followed Dr. Silver's advice and attended therapy sessions at the Hospital of God. The place either was an atheist parody of religion or indicated that God needed an interior designer. Its ceiling light fixtures provided a middle ground between mood lighting and headache-inducing dimness. The beige floors looked as if they'd been stolen from an early Soviet bunker. The building smelled like a mixture of antiseptic, prunes, and Vaseline. But at least the vertical row of gurneys on which three elderly patients, who would have seemed dead had they not snored like inebriated elephants, lay gave the place a sense that everything was going to be all right. Few things are more uplifting than viewing adult diaper changes. Try watching such a scene while listening to "Stop" by the Spice Girls, and your brain might shut down, as mine did.

I felt guilty for being jealous of the old folks' proximity to death. They probably would have relished the chance to return to their youths and relive periods in which life's possibilities seemed infinite, yet I was infatuated with putting myself in danger.

I still retained some hope of regaining control in another way. Even if the slightest glint of optimism hadn't manifested in my consciousness, I don't think I would have attended therapy if I'd been dead set on dying.

I arrived early and sat in the waiting room, which doubled as a staff kitchen. A doctor whose pants were about seven sizes too large filled a Styrofoam cup with coffee that lacked steam.

"Jacob Roth," a receptionist called.

"Yes, that is I. I am the sole patient in this room."

"Shelly is running a little late today. I will call you when she is ready."

I put my headphones back in my ears and listened to Jay-Z's "99 Problems." The lyrics distracted me from my surroundings. I was an emaciated, nerdy white teenager mouthing Jay-Z lyrics in the waiting room of an eating disorder clinic.

The delay was my week's most serene moment. I was oblivious to the surrounding chaos, allowing myself to get lost in the contents of my iPod and escape the depression. I tuned out the code blue and let my mind take a water break. "Tradition" from *Fiddler on the Roof* followed the Jay-Z playlist. I wondered what *Fiddler on the Roof*'s soundtrack would have sounded like if all its lyrics had been rapped. Such a thought was a refreshing change from the constant obsession with caloric intake.

After close to an hour's wait, the therapist summoned me to her office and apologized for her tardiness. Her name was Shelly. She was short and had an average build and long bright red hair. Her closet-sized office had two chairs, a desk, and some forgettable art on the wall.

At our first session, I outlined my background. I used humor to lighten a dark mood.

"Look, here's the skinny on what I'm going through. I don't eat. I fast for many days because I like the control that it gives me."

"Why?" she asked. Shelly sat upright in a cushioned chair.

"It gives me a sense of control. I know that is wrong. I've started changing it. I am here to change it."

I told Shelly about the feelings of isolation I'd experienced as a child.

"Why do you think you felt that way?"

"I have a theory about some kids in our generation. I think our parents and families tell us that we're all so amazing. Then we go out into the real world, and nobody else does. The truth is that most of us aren't special. Most of us are ordinary. Most of us will die, get buried, and be forgotten within a few generations. We won't even be a footnote of a footnote in the history of the world. That sounds dark, but I don't mean it that way—not at all. It's just the reality. I'm fine with that."

"Are you fine with that?"

"Yes, I'm completely fine with that. What I'm not fine with is the narrative that there's something wrong with the reality. That's where we go astray. Nobody outside of those who loved me told me I was special, because you know what? I wasn't. I couldn't handle negative feedback. It wasn't even negative feedback. I couldn't handle feedback that wasn't overwhelmingly positive. I couldn't handle normal childhood interactions. I convinced myself that I was different from everyone else."

"If that's a pattern with your generation, then why has it affected you seemingly more than others?"

"I guess that's my brain chemistry. I'm not equipped to deal with it."

"So you're here because you want to become better equipped to deal with your external environment."

"That's a reasonable way to characterize my presence."

"Here's what I'm going to recommend. Right now, we want to get you back to eating normally. I'm going to give you a food log. It's a sheet with a chart. Each box corresponds to a different time of the day. Write everything you eat in the food log."

She handed me the paper.

I was skeptical about the assignment. I worried that keeping a food log wouldn't normalize my eating. It would make me even more anxious about the number of calories I was consuming.

Shelly refuted my skepticism of her method by reminding me that I needed to formalize and systematize good habits. I was still concerned with the method, but rather than discussing it, I changed the topic to something light.

"So," I asked her suggestively, "you mean I write down everything that goes into my mouth? Everything?"

She was unimpressed when I joked that I was a gigolo. The cross that dangled from her thin silver chain stopped swaying. She didn't laugh. "I'll see you in a week, Jacob."

I left the Hospital of God with the chart in hand.

The next time I saw her, my body was weak from three consecutive days of shunning anything that had significant caloric content and wasn't phallus-shaped.

If a food item was low in calories and you could put a condom on it, I was eating it. I didn't notice the pattern at the time, but after reviewing my food log more recently, I spotted it. A day's meals would look something like this:

Breakfast: Banana
Morning snack: None
Lunch: Three pickles
Afternoon snack: Two baby carrots
Dinner: Half a cucumber and one zucchini
Evening snack: None

I still wonder whether Shelly ever noticed that my food log read like a porn set's grocery list or a game of dick, dick, nothing—the new anorexic duck, duck, goose. She asked me the standard questions that characterized our two sessions: How do you feel after you eat? How is debating? Have you won anything recently? How are your friends? Do you have any social plans outside of school? How is school? Are your grades staying high?

Therapy made me quiet and uncomfortable. I felt like Holden Caulfield, as I detested the therapist's phoniness. What would Shelly have said if she weren't in a stuffy office? Her questions and suggestions sounded as if they could have been traced to specific pages in textbooks: "Oh, you answered this. One second—let me check page 455 of my manual." She was like a paper fortune-teller to me. All I yearned for was genuine human connection. I would have welcomed advice on how to rid my mind of its destructive trespasser, but I knew that recovery wouldn't come from talking to a therapist whose behavior was textually determined. I wanted a friend, not a standardized procedure with a one-way dialogue. Therapy made me feel as if I were a subject to be studied and scrutinized. I was one of Shelly's hundreds of patients, and unless she had a photographic memory, she was going to forget about my existence.

That is not to say that she was a poor therapist or that therapy is fruitless. Shelly has probably helped many patients overcome their disordered eating. Nonetheless, entering her office transformed me into an introvert. If I couldn't ask Shelly about her life, then I didn't want to tell her about mine. I was uncomfortable with the idea that listening to my story was another hour to tack onto a paycheck. In each session, I felt as if I had mosquito bites running down my spine. Scratching would further irritate the itch, so beyond infrequent lewd allusions and some hints of skepticism, I was obedient. I responded to questions with the answers I thought Shelly wanted to hear.

"I am really motivated to get better, and I think I'm making progress," I lied. "This is the time."

Mendacity was the most efficient path to an early exit and gave my mind the freedom to travel elsewhere. I was like a bobblehead doll, pretending to agree with everything Shelly told me. She could have asked whether I would go on a drive-by with her, and I would have nodded.

I wanted to return to my apartment and shelter myself in a tub of self-pity. I wanted to pat myself on my bony back for losing more weight and cutting my already miniscule intake. I wanted to look at old family photos and remind myself that my best days were casualties of time. I wanted to sit alone at my desk and write about anything, from nonsensical ramblings to refined essays. I saw therapy as a monotonous break from my private rituals.

"Will I see you next week?" Shelly asked.

"Of course. I'll call your office to book an appointment when I know what my schedule looks like," I told her.

I was lying, for my second session with Shelly was the

last time I would seek professional help for my condition. As I left the hospital and walked out into the frigid Kingston winter, I knew I was going to retreat further into depression and solitude. My apartment was going to remain a shelter that I needed to escape to survive.

CHAPTER 16

O Holy Night

I want to go back. I want to go back. I want to go back. I want to go b—

I was twisting in my bed, reminiscing about winter holidays of the past. I use the word *holidays* because despite growing up Jewish, I was still part of a culture that celebrated Christmas and New Year's Eve according to the solar calendar. My favorite memories of this season are based not on its religious elements but on the extended opportunities to be with family and open presents. Material objects are the true meaning of the holidays, aren't they? *Happy birthday, Jesus. A hearty mazel tov on keeping that menorah going for eight days, Maccabees. Now, give me my new fucking* Mighty Machines *VHS. That's what I care about.*

In my dream, I was seven years old and at a restaurant in Boca Raton—or, as I call it, Israel Lite—with my parents, four grandparents, and Maddie. The speakers played Mariah Carey's rendition of "O Holy Night." Nana Sheila was complaining about the service. "Excuse me, but we've been waiting for our appetizers for more than ten minutes. And it's five thirty already, so it's really getting kinda late. Can you check on them, please? Thank you."

"Sheeeil. It'll come," Zaidy Paul said. "It's not a b—"

"Paul, this is ridiculous."

"Okay, okay, my dearest wife, whom I love more than anything in the world. Kids, are you ready to learn the next verse of 'Dirty Lil'?"

Nana glared at Zaidy Paul, prompting him to stop speaking—perhaps out of fear that she'd rip off a significant portion of his mustache.

Bubby was upset about the restaurant's temperature. "I think these places must coordinate with each other, because the air-conditioning is always blowing—constant blowing. It's frigid, and I'm wrapped in layers. S'cuse me." She motioned to the server. "Would it be possible to do something about the air-conditioning in here? It's really unbearable."

"Of course, ma'am."

He was lying.

When Bubby looked away, Zaidy Jerry snuck a slice of bread into his mouth, executing his strike with the precision of an NSA surveillance program, which is to say that he took a few more pieces than he should have and left some crumbs behind.

After dinner, Mom took me for ice cream. "Get as many scoops as you want to."

"Thanks, Mom."

"You know I'd do anything for my kids." She kissed my forehead.

I woke up and ripped the sheets off, stepped onto my snowy balcony, and stuck my head over the railing. Snowflakes fell and turned to water on my bony neck. I was shocked that I produced enough body heat to melt them.

"Should I jump off of this thing?" I asked the Anorexia God. "The ground is so tempting."

"Why would you do that?"

"I have to face my parents tomorrow. They are going

to lose it when they see how much I weigh. This could kill them."

"Talk about your marks instead. Be creative and get around the subject."

"That won't work. Health will trump school for them. Easily. So should I jump off this thing and end it all now? That would be way easier than the alternative."

"Do you believe that we have more to accomplish together?"

"Yes, I do—much more."

"Then there's your answer. You know what to do. You will figure it out."

I had never before been so frightened to see my parents. That year's holiday would not be some idyllic night in Israel Lite. The feigned smiles we'd slap on our faces would not conceal the hurt.

I arrived in Toronto on a snowy evening in the middle of December. Dad picked me up at the train station and drove me to our family's house. Slouching in the foyer, I removed my jacket and hoodie, revealing the skeleton underneath it.

"Holy shit, Jake," Mom said. "Are y—"

"What the hell happened?" Dad said before shielding his eyes from the skinny beast that greeted him. "For someone so smart, I can't believe you're doing this to yourself."

"Are you calling yourself smart, or is that just a dangling modifier?"

"Huh?"

"This is why I didn't want to come home. You're not being fair at all. It's always about weight, weight, weight.

I work out. Get over it. I'm really tired. I'm going to sleep. We'll talk tomorrow."

The yelling continued, but I ran upstairs and found a YouTube video of Mariah's "O Holy Night," which brought my mind back to the restaurant in Boca Raton. This time, the laughter and the innocence were gone. I imagined myself slumped over in a chair with blood gushing from my throat and abdomen while everyone shouted at me, the voices in my waking dream indistinguishable from the symphony of sadness.

"What the hell are you doing, Jake?"

"Our boy. Our boy."

"Jake."

"Please eat something."

"That's my grandson."

"Don't. D—"

"That's my son."

"You brought so much—"

"I'm a bad parent. I've failed you. I'm a—"

"Oh my God."

"This is not fair. What are you doing to yourself? Are you trying to sabotage everything?"

"You're ruining it all. You are—"

Nobody noticed that I hadn't taken a breath in hours, for they could react only to the visceral horror, not to the pain hidden behind my dying body. I guess when you first encounter the corpse of someone you love, your first response may not be to investigate the cause of death. You think, *Holy shit, Jake's dead.*

In Boca, Zaidy Jerry clanged his glass for a toast. "Can I have your attention for a minute? I want to say how happy I am to have us all here together. We are very fortunate that we get to have so many occasions like this one and that we are all here in good health, celebrating together. I can speak for Pearl too when I say how great it is to be with all of you: Paul and Sheila; our daughter; our son-in-law, who is like a son; and our two beautiful grandkids.

"I thank God for every day I can spend with all of you. Jake and Maddie, you have no idea how much joy you have brought and will continue to bring us. We are so proud of you. You are kind and compassionate, and you respect your friends. You do things the right way, Jake."

I still believed in the Anorexia God's promised rewards, yet my patience was fading like that of a child who could not wait to open a gift. My God was silent.

"So if everyone could raise his or her glass, I'll say l'chaim and here's to many, many more occasions like this one, and happy new year."

I noticed a cut on my wrist. But I couldn't identify its source. A few drops of blood landed on an assignment I had written, obscuring some of the words. The assignment was in the bathroom because I had brought it in to reread one night when I was lying there on the ground. Another speck of blood hit the brown tiles.

"Happy new year," they responded as their glasses clinked.

I didn't treat the wound and let it bleed for hours. Not dealing with the sting was a way to punish myself for destroying my family; it was my admission that I had chosen the Anorexia God above all else. I abhorred myself for harming those I loved. As the blood flowed, I envisioned how much better their lives would have been without me.

Dad greeted me the next morning. "What are you going to have for breakfast? You need to eat."

"I already ate. I was up early."

"Are you telling the truth? Like I said, I'll be very upset if you're not."

"You all are insane."

I was glad people worried about my skinniness but hated when my parents were the worriers. I wanted to shield them from my descent. They didn't deserve to suffer.

"Jake, this is serious. Your health matters. This is your future we're talking about."

"Why do you all assume dishonesty? Where are you getting all of this from?"

"Look at you. Please, for me, eat more, okay? Don't throw everything away."

"What exactly am I throwing away?"

"Your talent, your brilliant mind—your goddamn future."

"My mind is definitely not brilliant. I'm healthy. I'm working out, you know."

"Then eat more when you work out. I'd kill to have a mind like yours."

"No, you wouldn't. You're overstating my intelligence."

His forehead crinkled as if it were a discarded piece of paper. "Please eat more. For such a smart guy, I can't believe you're doing this. I really can't."

Similar scenes replayed for my entire two-week vacation. That was the first time I hated being with my family.

CHAPTER 17

No

January and Early February 2011

I was a half hour early for a boring class in the biological sciences building, a sprawling structure with scientific instruments I'm not smart enough to name. My classmate Liz was sitting at a food-court-style table with her friend, a thin brunette with wavy hair and dancer's legs.

I asked myself whether I should sit with them. *Should I hover around them so they feel bad and allow me to hang out with them? Should I do my own thing until class and let them have time to themselves? Could they be going over something super personal?*

I stopped the internal debate in my mind and decided to join them without requesting their permission.

I walked toward their table, trying to keep my right arm from dangling stupidly.

"Hey, may I join you?"

Liz nodded. I sat down at the table with them.

"This is my friend Tiffany. I've kind of told you about her. You guys are basically the exact same person. She doesn't drink. You don't drink. You're both into politics and that type of thing."

"Nice to meet you," I said, reaching my hand out to shake hers. "I—"

"You too," she replied, and she returned to the conversation that had begun before my arrival.

There wasn't anything magical about our first encounter.

"How's Baby Carrots?" Liz, who was clearly speaking in some sort of code, said to Tiffany.

"You know, all right," Tiffany said before making an incomprehensible sound effect.

"And Corn on the Cob. Corn on the Cob. Oh my God!" Liz howled.

"What about Nineteen? Do you remember Nineteen?"

They were speaking an unknown version of English, a sign that perhaps they wanted me to leave.

"Okay," I interjected, about to stand up, "I think I'm going to—"

"Where are you from?" Tiffany said.

The small talk led to a discussion through which Tiffany and I discovered similarities that made us compatible.

"Oh my goodness, you like throat music too," she said.

I'd never heard of throat music and soon learned that she had also fabricated her interest in the genre, yet that night, I listened to relevant albums so I would be able to boast about my expertise.

"People back where I'm from aren't really into throat music. I live in a really Jewish area where the regional sport is speed walking," I said.

"Are there, like, those guys who wear the cool black hats and have the really long beards?"

"You mean Chasidim?" I said. "Yeah, there are. They're very insular, kind of badass motherfuckers."

"That's so offensive. You shouldn't say those kinds of things."

"Seriously? I was totally kidding."

"No, it's really not nice to describe people that way. It's rude."

Great. I had known Tiffany for less than five minutes, but I had already offended her.

"Sorry. I didn't mean that comment to be offensive. I know some Chasidic people, and they are all very nice."

I want to include the following tip here: if someone accuses you of making insulting remarks, don't respond by bragging that you know people in the subject group.

"Are you in any clubs on campus?" Tiffany asked.

"I'm in the debating union. How about you?"

"I'm in Queen's Amnesty International. The debating union is so cool, dude. I thought about joining it for the longest time and took one of their pamphlets at orientation week, but I wouldn't have the guts to stand up there and all of a sudden debate like that, you know. I wouldn't be good at it either."

"Most people aren't good when they are new to competitive debating. It takes practice, and then you improve pretty rapidly. Moreover, even if you don't become a great debater, debating will help you become a better public speaker and organize your brain for essays."

"Oh my God. Did you actually use *moreover* in a sentence right now?"

Tiffany and Liz were both laughing at my formal diction.

"Yeah, what's wrong with that word?"

"Nothing is wrong with the word if you are in your seventies or writing an essay," Tiffany said. "*Moreover* is also one of my least favorite contraptions. It sounds so clumsy and silly."

"I think you mean *conjunction*, not *contraption*, but *moreover* is an adverb."

On the outside, I was laughing, yet I was angry with myself for using such a pretentious term.

I didn't initially think of Tiffany as more than a person with whom I'd shared twenty minutes, but to me, even a two-minute chat warranted Facebook friendship.

We started talking online and through text messages for hours at a time. She would playfully joke about my conception of *moreover* as a colloquial word.

"Whenever I hear someone use *moreover*, I actually think of how casually you use it."

"I used *moreover* in a debate at my tournament over the weekend. So it's working well."

The humor masked my embarrassment.

On a mid-February night that I'd have spent depressed and alone in my apartment, I invited myself to Tiffany's dorm, where, with Liz, we watched saccharine romantic comedies. By ten thirty, Liz was asleep, leaving my new friend and me in that uncomfortable phase of determining whether the guest should leave or stay longer. Tiffany interrupted the awkwardness, inviting me to stay longer by continuing a conversation I had initiated.

"You know I'm not going to tell you what *Baby Carrots* and all those words mean," she said pointing to an eight-and-a-half-by-eleven-inch sheet of paper on the wall above a night table. The page contained a collection of words that represented inside jokes she had with either Liz or her roommate, who was away for the weekend.

"Just tell me what you mean by *Baby Carrots*."

"No, I can't tell you that. It's a secret."

"Fine, then I will make fun of different religious groups, and you will be all offended."

"Then I'll call the school newspaper and tell them that Jacob Roth is a racist."

Surrounded by posters of punk rock bands whose members looked as if they wouldn't have any qualms about eating live humans onstage, I was wrapped in a blanket on her roommate's bed, continually adjusting myself to avoid the ceaseless frigidity that accompanied my anorexia.

"Do you think your roommate would care that I'm on her bed?"

"No, I don't think so."

"Good, because I have a bad case of lice."

While we talked until almost six o'clock in the morning, that night was like listening to a symphony. I appreciated a synthesis of numerous parts, but I could not identify each contribution. My recollection of those hours is minimal, an unusual failure of memory for a guy who remembers the name of his kindergarten teaching assistant's pet rabbit (Shlomo). Perhaps the shutdown of my mind's camera was its way of communicating that I needed to avoid overthinking and immerse myself in feeling the present. Or maybe I was exhausted, and there is neither a fancy nor romantic reason behind this aberration.

For a few days, I ate normal-sized meals, ignoring the Anorexia God and thinking about how I could muster the confidence to tell Tiffany how I felt about her.

A week had passed since I spent the night in her roommate's bed.

"Tonight is my time," I told myself. "You're going to tell

her, and you'll be smooth. Even if she thinks you're crazy, you will be persistent."

As I grew nervous about the prospect of rejection, the Anorexia God returned.

"Don't ask her on a date yet, Jake. You need to lose more weight. You ate like a non-ano all week. You've probably put on ten pounds. Stop eating, and then go for her."

I surrendered to the Anorexia God and fasted for two days before spilling my feelings into a text message.

I planned to ask Tiffany for advice about a made-up woman I was pursuing. That way, I would learn how she would want a guy to woo her.

"Hello. How are you?" I wrote, opening the thread.

"Ahaha, dude, you don't have to be so proper when you talk to me. You could be less formal. You're not writing an essay for me. Just stop."

"I always feel weird about being less formal, even in text messages. Such a formal conversational tone may make me a bit weird, but I posit that it is just my style. It's part of me."

"LOL *posit*. Okay, Mr. Professor."

"Yeah, I use *posit*. Anyway, I'm trying to ask this woman out and don't know how to go about it."

"Ahaha, which girl?"

"You don't know her. Her name is Michelle. How do I ask her? What's the best way?"

"Well, that depends on your relationship with her already. If it's kinda informal, like asking her on a date or something, you could text her or talk on Facebook. Just don't drag it out. Be up front. You can defs keep things simple."

"What if she says no?"

"Then she says no, and there's nothing you can do about it other than try harder or give up, I guess."

"Hmm, I suppose you are correct. Should I write her a letter?"

"Aha, a letter could be nice, but I dunno. It could be too formal. It may freak her out a bit."

"Thanks for the advice. I think I'll bring it up in a text message. That's the simplest way to do it."

"LOL. Let me know how it goes."

"Btdubs, you're Michelle."

In an attempt to portray myself as young and hip, I used *btdubs*, slang that is popular among ten- to twelve-year-olds. I was that inept.

"Dude, I'm sorry I don't feel the same way about you. I really value your friendship, and I hope that will continue, but that's all there is. I see you as a really good friend. That's all. Sorry."

"Okay, good night."

I stared at the phone. If I hadn't had the strength of an orthodox anorexic, my tight grip would have crushed the device.

Pondering how I could persuade Tiffany to reciprocate, I stayed up until the early morning.

"Be persistent," my friend Ari said. "Don't take the first no for an absolute final answer. Try a few more times. Invite her over, and let her get to know you. I mean, you've known this girl for, what, like less than a month? So you could have possibly freaked her out a bit by moving so fast. Give it a little bit more of a shot."

At least thirty-seven trillion times, I asked Tiffany over to my apartment for a date.

"Dude, you need to stop asking. I don't like you in that way. Please stop already."

"No, I'm not going to stop unless you file a restraining order against me."

"Don't tempt me. If I go on this date or whatever you want to call it, will you stop asking?"

"Yes, if you give me one chance and you still feel the same way, then I will give up."

"Fine, I'll come this Saturday. Don't get your hopes up, though."

Saturday

I dedicated more than ten hours to cleaning my apartment. The place had already been almost spotless, but it needed to shine for Tiffany. I scoured everything, removing all the forks from the drawer, the plates from the cupboard, and the burners from the stove to ensure that every crevice was sparkling. I refolded clothes, puffed cushions, scrubbed the sink and shower, vacuumed the carpet four times, squeegeed the windows, and wiped off the kitchen table and counters. Once everything was shining like Miss Hannigan's orphanage, I showered and then dressed in a plaid button-down shirt with blue jeans. I even brushed my hair.

When Tiffany warned me that she would arrive in twenty minutes, I started cooking pasta and warming jarred tomato sauce. Far from Gordon Ramsay in the kitchen, I spilled half the jar of sauce on my shirt. I changed into a plaid alternative because, as Mom claimed, that was "the look the kids are wearing these days."

I put the pasta in a plastic bowl and set the table with two white cup candles.

"Here," Tiffany's text message read.

I met her in the lobby. Because she was petrified of elevators, we climbed the nine flights of stairs to my apartment.

Aside from my spilling pasta everywhere on the table, the date began perfectly. I learned about her passion for water policy and her dream of becoming a personal assistant. We made fun of our parents, and we laughed at her sixty thousand phobias and my formal personality.

"So if we became a couple, we would go to all sorts of—"

"Dude, we're not going to become a couple because I don't like you in that way. That's solved."

"Okay, whatever you say. But hey, if we became a couple, we'd have kids who spoke in full sentences and were afraid of dogs, highway traffic, elevators, swimming, airplanes, the dark, sheep, clowns, and public speaking. Those sound like pretty normal kids."

By midnight, Tiffany was asleep on the couch.

When I walked her about a mile back to her dorm at five thirty in the morning, I thought I had wooed her.

"Thanks for the best date," she said as we stood outside her building.

"So can we schedule another one?"

"No, I had a good time, but I still feel the same way. Sorry. I even tried to get myself to like you. I really, really did try. It's just not there for me. You're a nice guy and all, but you're not my type."

"What is your type?"

"I don't want to be mean about it. It's not fair if you ask me. Don't make me answer that, please."

"Tell me anyway. I won't care. I'm tough."

"I don't know. I guess I want a guy with a little more swag than you have."

"What is swag? Is it something you wear?"

"It's something you don't have. I still like you as a friend. Don't worry."

"It's okay. I'll keep trying."

"Please stop trying. You said you'd stop after the date. You don't have a chance."

As she disappeared into her residence, I stood alone and worried that the winter morning sun would burn the back of my neck. The world was blurry.

I took a cab back to my apartment, where nothing had moved. Tomato sauce was hardening on the dinner plates, which were still on the table. The couch cushion on which she'd slept had not moved. My laptop, which had displayed *Jesus Camp* a few hours earlier, was still open and perched at the end of the black IKEA coffee table.

The stillness reminded me of how quickly misery could shatter happiness. My apartment's contents were teasing me. My outburst was a collision of negative emotions. Whether because of Tiffany or another external source, a tantrum was inevitable.

I slammed my open palm on the kitchen table, which caused a plate and cutlery to fall to the floor.

"See? I told you." The Anorexia God chuckled.

I was hyperventilating. "Fuck off. Not now," I said. "Don't be a piece of shit."

"You're not good enough for her. No swagger. I was right. You shouldn't have eaten two plates of pasta on the date. And you definitely shouldn't have eaten anything before your date. What were you thinking?"

"I'm sorry. You're right. I was wrong. I was wrong. I was wrong."

"You finally admit it."

"I thought I could take a break and maybe could live normally or actually have some control over my life. I am imperfect. I'm really flawed. I screwed up. What should I do?"

"That's just the thing, Jake. You are not normal. You will never be normal. You should never try to be normal. The sooner you adopt your identity as an anorexic, the sooner the world will become clear to you."

"That's not really a concrete solution to my problem. What should I do right now? What will make me feel better?"

"You could fast until you die."

"That would be too painful."

"What about swallowing a bottle of pills and killing yourself? You have Tylenol in your bathroom. Your mother left it there."

"No, I couldn't do that to my family. That would be way too cruel. I'm not even sure Tylenol would finish the job. Maybe one day I will change my mind, but I wouldn't be brave enough to take such a step now."

"Okay, then start with fasting until Thursday night."

I obeyed the Anorexia God, drinking nothing but water for five consecutive days. The hunger made me dizzy, yet the physical symptoms didn't rival the pain in my mind.

To prevent myself from swallowing a bottle of pills, I opened a text message conversation with Maddie. I needed to talk to someone who wouldn't think of me as a burden and who would respond calmly. Maddie could demonstrate her affection without bewailing my condition. After the pleasantries gave way to an inquiry about my health, I spilled the accumulated sadness onto my cell phone.

"I'm miserable. I really hate myself. I met this woman,

Tiffany, and we went on a date. I like her and thought that things were going pretty well, but she doesn't feel the same way. Am I being stupid? Maybe. But what I'm feeling isn't solely about her. I hate myself. I've eaten maybe a few pickles and apples this week and am becoming really weak. I have been dizzy all the time. It's not good."

"Do you want to talk to Mom or Dad?"

"No."

"Do you think you need to come home?"

"No, I'm not going to waste a semester."

"Who is this Tiffany person?"

"I met her through a mutual friend. She and I are really similar. Neither of us does drugs or drinks. Well, alcohol. We have really similar interests. She's nerdy but not in a geeky or all-consuming way. I mean, she has intellectual interests outside of school. Anyway, I've been trying to get her to go out with me for a while now, and she agreed to go on a date with me—maybe out of pity (who knows, right?). Everything seemed to be going well, and then the next day, she said she still saw me as a friend. I was really upset. I'm always sad. I know my reaction wasn't really about Tiffany's rejection. It was about another failure at a time when I think that everything is failing me."

"Well, if this Tiffany chick doesn't see it in you, then maybe she's not right for you."

"No, I don't blame her. I'm not fun to be around."

"That's not true. You're one of the smartest and nicest people I've ever met. Trust me on that. Ask my friends. They all think you're smart and funny and caring. You need to see that in yourself. You're fooling yourself into believing you're this, like, bad person. I don't have half of what you have."

"That's nice of you to say, but you are either biased or haven't met enough smart people."

"I'm worried about you, Jake."

"There's no need to worry. My situation is life, I guess. Shitty things happen. Please promise me you won't tell Mom and Dad about any of this. I don't want to kill them. They'd lose it."

"I promise."

"Perhaps one day I'll write a book about my eating disorder experiences, and they'll hear about it then. Really, you can't tell them anything. These messages don't exist. Please delete them."

"I will. Don't worry about it."

"Good night. Thanks for listening—er, reading."

"Please get better, and maybe eat a tiny bit more if you can for me, please."

Our ancient sibling rivalry prohibited an "I love you," yet the sentiment was palpable. For a few minutes, Maddie had been a painkiller, allowing me to forget about the loneliness. However, when the conversation ended and I gazed at the filthy dishes that snuck through the night's darkness, the depression smothered me again.

"I want to make sure you don't listen to your sister's last message," the Anorexia God said. "This feeling will get worse if you eat more. She's telling you to get fat."

"I agree."

"It's okay to hate yourself."

"You're right."

"Good. Beyond your anorexia, you are nothing. You have very little to offer the world. At best, you are average, a blob of meh."

"I agree."

For the rest of the week, the date's debris lay strewn across the floor. My apartment smelled of old tomato sauce.

CHAPTER 18

The Mirror

February

I was in the midst of a nightmare.

"Help! Bloody help!" a voice said in the distance. "Help!"

"Where are you? What's wrong?" I asked.

"I'm right here. I just need help. I am bleeding, man. I am bleeding. I am—"

Although the voice seemed to be getting closer, I couldn't locate it.

"I'm dying. Holy shit, dude. I'm dying. You'd better come quickly. You'd better come now. Please."

I was sprinting toward a nonexistent target.

"Are you coming? I am bleeding. I am bleeding. I—"

I chased the voice of the invisible victim, not once slowing to catch my breath.

"Are you coming? Help me. What's taking so long?"

"I am trying, sir. I can't find you. Where are you? I hear you, but I can't find you anywhere."

"I am right here, right under your fingertips."

"What's your name?" I asked him.

"It's Gantry. My name is Gantry."

The voice was in front of me, yet the man wasn't there.

"I'm dying. I'm dying!" he cried. "I need your help. Or could you at least call somebody?"

Like a horse chasing an ever-moving carrot on a stick, I was sprinting toward an unreachable destination. An intense gust of wind blew away the cell phone I had removed from my jacket pocket.

"I'm sorry," I told him. "I am really sorry, Gantry. I really can't run any longer."

"Do you love me?" he asked. "Please tell me you love me. I don't want to die alone."

"Yes, Gantry. I love you," I sobbed. "I love you. I—"

Out of breath, I collapsed to the ground. I was powerless to save Gantry from his imminent death.

A light drop of a mysterious red liquid landed on my forehead. Before I could identify what it was, a downpour of blood and guts soaked my body. As I wiped a piece of a heart out of my eyes, I noticed a dog tag resting at my feet. It read, "Gantry."

I woke up. The realism of Gantry's death left me with a sinking feeling in my stomach. Gantry symbolized my perceived powerlessness. He was right in front of me, yet I couldn't reverse the outcome that neither of us wanted.

I was bundled in three sweatshirts and four blankets. Panting, I stripped off all my upper body's clothing and felt the part of my stomach where there was an unacceptable patch of fat. I ripped off the sheets and ran to the full-length mirror on the westernmost wall of the apartment.

Wearing nothing but boxer shorts, I stood in front of the mirror and examined almost every aspect of my exposed body. I needed to reduce the size of my stomach. Oh my goodness, did I have man tits? Were my legs chunky? I must have had four chins, at least double what I'd seen last time

I'd studied myself. My face was chubby, and my fingers were way too thick. The images in the mirror were horrifying. I couldn't believe the hideousness that shot back at me. Every part of my body was flawed.

What I saw in the mirror wasn't real. It reflected my warped perceptions. The looking glass had artistic license to change the figure standing in front of it. A mouse could have become a giraffe. I saw not the true picture but what the Anorexia God wanted to show me. He was telling me that I needed to submit further. Since I had not lost much weight in the few weeks prior, I was required to cut more from my diet.

At 4:02 a.m., I jumped back into bed, but I couldn't sleep, as thoughts of anorexic failure flooded my mind. My eyes wouldn't remain shut for more than a few minutes at a time.

My current weight was offensive to me, which meant I needed a plan to become even thinner. I had to show the Anorexia God that I was devoted to him. Doubt could not interfere with my unconditional piety.

Sitting underneath a flickering lamp, I compiled criteria for consumption:

- maximum of 195 calories per food item
- no more than 2.1 grams of fat
- no more than 475 calories per day
- more than 300 calories requires 20 minutes of running stairs or equivalent cardio

My new plan was supposed to clean the filth in the mirror. The ugliness of the present would be tolerable if it yielded a beautiful future.

I accepted that these new restrictions could kill me.

Running stairs and stressing my cardiovascular system with such minimal nutrition could be fatal. I expected that one day my apartment building's superintendents might find me dead in the stairwell or my apartment. They'd potentially have to call a trauma scene cleanup crew to peel my rotting and foul-smelling corpse from the ground. Somebody would stuff me in a wooden box and then lower me into eternal obscurity.

To most people, such an ending would be undesirable, but after looking in that mirror, I concluded that sacrificing myself to the Anorexia God was how I wanted to die. I had the opportunity to terminate my existence in pursuit of what I saw as the purest form of consciousness. It would be martyrdom.

That ending seemed appropriate. I dreamed about breathing my last breaths and feeling the sense of accomplishment that had always eluded me.

I lifted my shirt and felt a layer of nonexistent fat on my stomach. This time, however, I was optimistic that the fat would soon disappear.

I was flirting with my mortality and wondering how long it would take to accept my advances.

CHAPTER 19

Five-Day Fast

Day One

The next day, in my first-year politics tutorial, the teaching assistant was handing back marked essays to the students. I was arrogant and expected to get an A on the assignment. I thought the creative flare I'd added to my paper should have distinguished it from the dryness that the graders were accustomed to reading. My ridiculous and corny introduction read as follows:

> "Titan Spirit" reverberated through Chicago's Grant Park amid a spectacle of hope, bipartisanship, change, and reaffirmed democratic ideals. President-Elect Barack Obama, whose campaign transformed a divided country into a nation, delivered his trademark creed: "Yes we can." But since the president marched on Pennsylvania Avenue, the galvanized and unified America he produced has reverted into a state of division and mistrust in the office for which he took an oath.

I didn't score an A on the assignment.

"Jacob," the TA wrote, "your analysis on this assignment is very good. However, at times, it comes across as a bit of a polemic. Your writing style may work well journalistically or creatively. Unfortunately, it is not always academic. In future papers, you could try to use more of an academic tone in your essays, and it will read much better. A-."

In retrospect, I think that TA gave me the most useful advice I received in all my years at university. Had the minus been taken away from the A, I would have appreciated the comment, but that minus, that worthless and pathetic symbol at the end of my paper, was unacceptable.

"You're an idiot," the Anorexia God said as we walked back to my apartment on a snowy afternoon. I was shivering beneath my coat and layers of sweaters. "An A- is a joke. You are a joke."

"I know I am. What should I do about it?"

"Well, you haven't yet eaten today, which is really good."

"I know. I'm going to fast for a few days. Are there any other solutions?"

"Try fasting for five days starting today, and let's see how successful that winds up being."

We returned to my apartment, where everything and nothing had changed since my failed date with Tiffany. Plates were still in fragments on the floor, the cutlery was still strewn across the place, and jagged glass was still waiting to be swept or vacuumed.

I opened the linen closet and threw all my shirts onto the carpet.

"Goddammit. A-. Shit. That's pitiful!" I yelled.

I punched the wooden closet door, but my anorexic strength wasn't enough to even dent it.

"Shit," I said again, looking at the essay. "A-. What the hell is wrong with you? You're an idiot."

A shirt that was dangling from a hanging rack fell to the ground.

I ripped the paper into thousands of pieces before throwing its remnants in the air as if they were ironic confetti.

"Jake, you will feel better in a few days. You just need to give your body a good cleanse. You had too much food on the date with Tiffany. You know that. You couldn't have cared about the date given how much you ate," the Anorexia God said.

As the sun set, I was ready to consume only water for another four days.

Day Two

"Are you okay?" an early-morning text message from Tiffany read.

"Yes, I'm fine. Why do you ask?"

"I dunno. I haven't heard from you in a couple of days. I was just wondering."

"Yeah, I'm fine, but hey, I know you enjoyed that date, and you still like me, so don't deny it."

"Dude, I don't like you in that way. When are you going to stop thinking that?"

"Never, because I know you just can't admit what's in front of you. If you didn't like me, you wouldn't have stayed so late that night and talked about life for so long."

"Whatever you say, dude."

"Whatever I say is right."

Three hours passed, yet she had not responded to my

most recent message. *Did I push her too far? Was I too aggressive? Should I not have put feelings in her mind? Why am I incompetent?*

Even in class, I would not put down my cell phone, for I hoped I would hear something—anything—from Tiffany. I was obnoxiously overbearing, yet I didn't want to be super obnoxiously overbearing, so I promised myself I would not send her another message until she replied.

I didn't think about my lack of nutrition once during my three consecutive classes. Despite having shunned food for more than twenty-four hours, I wasn't at all hungry. I listened to my professors and took notes as if my routine were normal. Every few minutes, however, I grabbed the lower half of my stomach to check for new fat patches. Was the fast working? Was I losing the large gut that my brain invented every time I looked in the mirror?

In the early evening, while I was staring out at the snow-covered roads from the window of my ninth-floor apartment, my phone vibrated.

"How were your classes today?" Tiffany wrote.

I was relieved that she remembered me. "Good. Do you want to go on another date soon?"

"Dude, you need to stop trying that. I like being your friend, but please stop trying to get me to go on more dates with you. It's not fair to you and not fair to me."

"Why isn't it fair? I know that you would like to go on another date. Admit it."

"No, I really don't want to. I'm sorry."

"Don't lie."

"I'm not lying. Sorry you're not my type."

"Yeah, I know that you want a guy with swagger—whatever that means."

"Not just swag, but I like tall guys, and they should also be muscular. You're neither of those things. Sorry."

I let the phone fall to the couch, on which I was lying with my feet up. Like a car crashing full speed into a traffic barrier, Tiffany's words slammed into my already vulnerable mind. I closed my eyes, not to sleep but to shield them from the light until my alarm clock rang at seven o'clock the next morning.

Day Three

When I awoke, I was dizzy from hunger. The bed was spinning, sporadically alternating between clockwise and counterclockwise. A plump Granny Smith apple was slouching on the coffee table in front of the couch. Its shiny green skin invited me into its juicy flesh. I could taste its sourness and feel its hard exterior meeting my teeth.

"Don't even think about it," the Anorexia God said. "You're contemplating getting fat. You want to get fat."

I picked up the apple, feeling its roundness in my palms, and then rubbed it against my cheeks.

"It's like one hundred twenty calories, and the dietary fiber would fill me for a long time. Maybe I should just eat it," I said to the Anorexia God. "It wouldn't be so bad."

"Don't even take one bite. You know what will happen. One bite of an apple here, and *boom*—you're advocating having a second and then throwing in some lentils and a protein drink. What you're proposing is giving up on something you want. If you can't do this, then you can't do anything."

"Don't you know that a slippery slope is a logical fallacy?"

"Yeah, but this is not fallacious. You are anorexic. Your personality lends itself to the kind of argument we would associate with the slippery-slope fallacy. You do one thing, like lose a little bit of weight, and then all of a sudden, you're dropping thirty pounds, then forty, and then fifty, and you're going all the way. You're worshipping me, after all."

"You are right. I shouldn't have even considered it."

"You know I have your best interests in mind, Jake."

"That's why I love you."

I allowed the apple to continue resting on the table, ignoring its constant invitations and letting my stomach grumble. The promise of eternal rewards made the physical pain tolerable. I was aware that the road to a glorious future would feature obstacles that would challenge my faith.

For the remainder of the day, temptations stalked me. My first class was in a building with a food court. The psychedelic smell of the pizza with its melting processed cheese and sodium-rich crust mocked me for what I could not have. Every corner of every room teased me with different sources of cravings. Food was omnipresent. Between my right thumb and index finger, I pinched imaginary flabs of belly fat to reassure myself that I was chasing a worthwhile objective. I had shed mass, yet my project remained incomplete. My bodily imperfections persisted. Drowning in the scents of sin, I vowed to continue my strict observance to the Anorexia God.

My frustration surfaced in a morning tutorial discussion. I was in a class with about twenty students. The classroom could have seated forty people. An androgynous teaching assistant was ranting in front of an empty chalkboard. The bald teaching assistant was wearing a white long-sleeved shirt with a picture of a fist on it and the word *Resist* written above the image.

"Let's talk about people of color in film. There aren't enough black individuals in film," the TA said. "There shouldn't be such a thing as a white role or a black role. Every actor should be qualified to play any character, and we must end race-selective auditions. There's no such thing as a black role or a white role. We shouldn't see race at all, so even historical characters could be played by any actor, regardless of color."

I thought the TA was establishing unreasonable expectations.

"Comments?" the TA said.

I raised my hand. "Yeah, you're right that inequalities exist and are pernicious, but your solution doesn't work. That is, unless you think Sean Penn would be a compelling Malcolm X, Denzel Washington would be an awesome Oskar Schindler, and Jackie Chan would make the perfect Mahatma Gandhi."

"Sometimes racial equality is more important than movies are," the TA said. "You shouldn't be close-minded. Who says Denzel Washington couldn't be an awesome Oskar Schindler?"

"Why can't Hollywood be equitable without compromising the integrity of art?"

"You like to challenge things, don't you? I recall last week you also said that asking somebody about their background wasn't racist. It's a good thing you're taking this course. You have a lot to learn, Jacob. You have some pretty vile viewpoints. You are perpetuating an aggressive white-supremacist colonial-settler mentality."

I wanted to throw my pen at the chalkboard, but I was afraid the TA would construe its blueness as racist.

"Yeah, if I politely ask from where someone's accent derives, I'm vicious."

"Why are we having this debate in the twenty-first century? You might as well be using a racial slur, Jacob."

"I think learning about a person's background can be nice and enriching. That doesn't mean being rude about it in a 'Where the hell are you from?' manner, but if I am genuinely curious about an individual, asking is a sign of consideration. Tone matters."

"It's cruel and racist. If you really believe that asking one about background isn't deeply harmful, then you are racist yourself. What you are saying is actually quite vicious. It's more than problematic. It's horrific. You're a white supremacist."

"I see somewhat of a reasonable case for your argument, but to call a polite inquiry vicious and akin to a slur? I mean, come on. Really? You could argue that maybe asking about someone's background presents problems. But to shoot for the moon of descriptors by calling me a white supremacist is so beyond the pale of reasonable discourse. It demeans the gravity of the term and those whom white supremacy has victimized."

While I was annoyed that the teaching assistant was instructing the class to hate the past, present, and future, I think my sarcastic outburst derived from my hatred of my life. I've made it my life's mission to avoid burning bridges, so that outburst was out of character.

Before the TA could boot me from the class, I'd logged in to my online student account and dropped the course. I was proud and surprised that I had defended myself.

Standing right outside the battlefield I had left, I noticed an unread text message on my phone.

"Would you like to join Liz and me for lunch in a few minutes?" Tiffany asked.

Her invitation presented an obvious problem. I was tied to the five-day fast. I would need to convince Tiffany I'd eaten a substantial lunch right before I opened her note.

The cafeteria was an all-you-can-eat buffet, so I had to pay an entrance fee. The real investment was in the time I would have with Tiffany.

"Aren't you going to get something to eat?" she said when I sat down beside Liz and her at the table.

"No, I already ate a big lunch."

She didn't press me to eat something else. I don't know whether Tiffany believed my lie or just wanted to avoid a debate with me.

Tiffany and Liz were speaking in code again.

"Freddie is being such a douche."

"Just like his friend Nineteen. What a dick."

"What's stalker boy been up to lately?"

"Not much. He's been pretty good."

I ignored both the unintelligible conversation and the food, which would have ridiculed my senses minutes ago. The latter had ceased being enticing. I fixated on Tiffany instead. She was wearing the T-shirt of a band I didn't know and one of her many pairs of American Eagle jeans. Her deep brown eyes, immature smile, and childish laugh transported my mind back to the rotting tomato sauce. I needed the feelings to be mutual or to believe I had a sliver of a chance to make her feel, if not butterflies, caterpillars in her stomach.

"Oh, Jake, you are a moron," the Anorexia God groaned. "You're quite the dreamer, aren't you? A hapless romantic."

"Not really. I haven't even uttered a word to her at this table. I should try that."

"Try all you want. It ain't going to work. Focus on your fast."

"Tiffany is distracting me from the fast."

"Then you don't want anything out of your life. You shouldn't be distracted from the fast. Food-related temptation is a good thing. Seeing and smelling food everywhere is also useful. It makes your anorexia more meaningful, more of an accomplishment, ya know. If you're not thinking about why you're losing weight, then you're not achieving the most beautiful kind of control. You're having one half of the experience."

"Who is Nineteen?" I asked Tiffany and Liz.

"Don't worry about it," Tiffany answered.

"But I am worried about it. I want to know who it is."

"Nineteen is the number after eighteen and before twenty."

"That's a crock of shit. What does it really mean?"

"It's not a crock. It actually just means that. It's a number. That's all."

"Then it wouldn't make sense in the context you just used it in."

"It makes sense. Trust me."

"I think it has something to do with men."

Tiffany and Liz giggled as if I had solved a mystery for which they would not provide further clues.

"Tiffany, you should go on another date with Jake," Liz said.

I was unsure whether Liz was being sarcastic. Feeling uncomfortable, I moved the chat back to deciphering the code. They soon left for their classes, leaving me alone to murder time in a cafeteria teeming with gustatory temptations.

The rest of the day was forgettable. To avoid hunger pains, I fell asleep at five thirty that evening and didn't awake until late the next morning.

Day Four

I went to an hour-long class at eleven o'clock and then returned to my apartment, where I slept for most of the afternoon, evening, and night. My body was hurting. A construction crew was pounding the inside of my head, a porcupine was shooting its quills through the lower half of my spine, and a boxer was pulverizing my face. My bedsheets sheltered me from the pain. I sought complete isolation from the rest of the world. I lied to my parents, telling them I was in lectures and debating meetings all day, and then took out the batteries from both my landline and cell phone. My bedroom door was closed, and the blinds were shut. I preserved the gorgeous darkness by wearing earplugs to block any outside noise and a sparkly pink sleep mask with a picture of a cupcake on it. Without provoking my attention, my neighbors could have spent the entire day at the zoo.

By four thirty in the afternoon, I was asleep for the night.

Day Five

My eyes reopened late in the afternoon.

"Jake, congratulations. Well done," the Anorexia God said. "Mazel tov. You're very close to the five-day point."

"Yeah, I am, but my body feels like that of a lactose-intolerant person who just had sixty-five bowls of ice cream."

"I know the fast is hard. You also knew this would be challenging, and it has been. But aside from the physical discomfort, how do you feel?"

"I feel absolutely amazing."

Dizzier than a drunk on an upside-down roller coaster, I stumbled toward the mirror, where I removed everything but my boxers. I littered the floor with three sweaters, an undershirt, long underwear, and three pairs of sweatpants. My reflection in the mirror was blurry, but I could still see disappointment screaming back at me.

"How, after almost five days of fasting, are my thighs still chunky? How is my belly not flat? How do I have so many chins?"

"Easy answer," the Anorexia God said. "Do you think that a five-day mini-fast is all you need? You had a few normal meals last week. This five-day fast is a good start for sure, but you're going to have to do more soon. And even when the fast is over, you won't be able to go eat whatever you want. Have a banana, an apple, or some vegetables, and maybe once a week, you could have a veggie dog. You can't all of a sudden return to normal eating. You have to be strong—very strong. Your journey will not always be straightforward."

"I know it will be difficult. Still, I thought I'd see something better than this grotesque image in the damn mirror."

"It is pretty grotesque. I will definitely agree with you on that one."

A current of vomit moved from my stomach to my throat. I scampered to the bathroom, opened the toilet's lid, and crashed to my knees. Blood and mucus struck the bowl as if they were falling from a water-park attraction. As sweat tumbled down my cheeks, my upper body swung. When I thought I had nothing left to puke, my mouth opened, and more liquid followed.

An indefinable amount of time passed. I would not have recognized the difference between five minutes and nine hours.

Nonetheless, I remember that after the vomiting stopped, I sat shirtless with my back against the damp wall and wiped away the perspiration with a soggy washcloth. I glared at my stomach roll.

"I should probably see a doctor about the blood in my throw-up."

"Don't be such a pussy all the time," the Anorexia God said.

I crawled to the kitchen, where I chewed on both a banana and God's words, trying to avoid accepting them without further contemplation.

CHAPTER 20

One Night in a Sticky Motel

February 2011

I was in Waterloo, a small city just more than three hours west of Kingston, for a debating tournament.

Our motel smelled like an abandoned colonoscopy clinic that had been transformed into an alcohol-soaked swingers' club. I could feel the rattling heater lifting DNA from the duvet and filling the room with blood, urine, and semen. That night's guest list of university debaters was evenly split between johns and prostitutes. It was what I called the Traditional Values Coalition's wet nightmare.

Katherine, Adam, and I were lying on a double bed only a masochist would have ever run a black light over. Katherine wore a light blue long-sleeved top and black leggings that fit her figure-skater physique. Her black hair hung a few inches below her shoulders. Adam was in blue jeans and a gray T-shirt. His Jew-fro dwarfed the white pillowcase.

A day of debating about international affairs, feminist utopias, Harry Potter, and domestic economics had given way to boozy conversations about nothing and everything. Despite my sobriety, I was, as usual, the drunkest person in the room. I don't drink, but if I am awake past eleven o'clock, I might as well be smashed.

It was one forty-five in the morning.

"I want to start a business," I said.

"Oh yeah?" Adam asked as if he knew that my next line was going to be absurd.

"Yeah, I've always wanted to buy a hearse and turn it into an ice cream truck. Well, I guess it would be more of an ice cream hearse than a truck. You get the point."

"You're sick, eh. I mean, you're a total lunatic."

"Why is that such a bad idea? It would be ice cream to die for."

"Puns are the lowest form of humor." He rolled his eyes.

"What if I call it Cream-ations?" I said. "Get it?"

"Oy."

"What do you think, Katherine?"

Katherine lowered the drink from her mouth. "Um, I mean, I guess if you think it's a good idea, then go for it, sure," she said. "You're better off pursuing that rap career. What's your stage name again?"

"DJ Skinny."

"Right. That's perfect."

"Would you invest in my business?" I asked. "You're dying to do it, aren't you?"

Adam, while finishing the final drops of a drink, agreed. He was enthusiastic about the idea. Katherine shook her head, a nonverbal indication that she didn't know how to respond to my zaniness.

"Wow, Katherine. That's so anti-Semitic. Are you just avoiding going into business with Adam and me because we are Jewish? I'm going to call the *Canadian Jewish News*, and they'll plaster your name as a hater on their front page. You'll be right on the front page."

Adam and I both tried to make Katherine apologize for such a stance. That was our shtick. Somebody would say something benign, yet Adam and I would call the statement racist or anti-Semitic and demand an apology. It was our way of bothering our peers.

For hours, Adam, Katherine, and I continued to talk about nonsense. I made way too many references to and puns about my circumcision. We poked fun at other members of the debating union, including Willow, an exchange student who admitted she was sexually attracted to her brother. Adam and Katherine even allowed me to laugh at my eating disorder. I was comfortable with them. I typically deliberated about the jokes I'd tell. Humor was a calculation, a way to carefully determine how my words would affect people's perceptions of me: Jesus reference + self-depreciation = laugh = positive social outcome. But I felt as if Adam and Katherine were my old friends. They allowed my mind to work freely.

More importantly, I hadn't known Adam and Katherine for long. I had grown these relationships within a few months, which offered me a sliver of self-confidence. On that night in the sticky motel, I forgot about my fascination with death. I thought not about the past but about the prospects for the future. Adam and Katherine could be concerned about my eating disorder while also finding humor in my DJ Skinny pseudonym and avoiding an all-encompassing focus on the emaciated bag of bones in front of them. As I watched the sun rise over the empty-beer-bottle-filled parking lot of a cheap Waterloo motel, a passing desire to live interrupted my self-hatred.

"You know what I want to do?" I said. "I want to buy anal beads, put a clasp on them, and give them as a gift to a woman. I bet a million dollars she'll say, 'Aw, that's so sweet. What a nice bracelet.' I should totally do that."

"Go for it, Jake. We should totally get you drunk," Adam said. "It has to happen."

"That's a horrible idea. I'd probably wind up running down the street while wearing assless chaps and a large gold chain with a Jewish star and screaming, 'The gods must be crazy!' Why would I even get drunk? I'm already completely nuts, ya know."

"Yeah, well, you don't eat, and that's kinda already nuts," Adam said. "You should eat food. It's tasty, and some of it is really good for you."

"It couldn't be nuts," I said. "Nuts have too many calories."

Adam laughed. I stopped talking for a few minutes to let myself consider that I had friends who found humor in my condition. They were interested in what I had labeled my dreary personality. I attributed that triumph to my anorexia. It constructed my confidence and made me socially marketable. Until they fell asleep, Adam and Katherine seemed to enjoy my company.

"You see?" the Anorexia God said. "This is happening because of the project that we've undertaken together. You should be very proud of yourself. Your job is not over, yet you have conquered a major phase of this process. Rest well tonight."

I looked over at my two sleeping friends. They probably would not have minded if I'd drawn on their faces.

CHAPTER 21

The Gates

The next morning, I woke up sad. I hadn't forgotten about those few hours in the sticky motel, but happiness was gone before I could even enjoy its clarity.

I was alone. Katherine and Adam had left to fetch coffee in the lobby before heading to the campus on which the tournament's final rounds would take place. The empty bottles in the recycling bin reminded me of comfort's elusiveness. I was too depressed to extricate myself from the bed. The dirty sheets and folded pillows sheltered me from facing the world in such a state.

I called the front desk to request an extended checkout.

"Hello," I said almost inaudibly. "Could I possibly extend the time I have on this room until later this afternoon? I'd pay for it, of course."

"That's no problem. Just come down to the front desk when you're ready to check out."

I hung up the phone as if it were smoldering and covered my face with the linens.

"Jake, are you coming to the tournament soon?" my debating friend WuDi Wu texted me.

"Nah, I think I've come down with a cold, so I'm going

to rest a bit. Text me when it's almost over, so I can meet you guys in the parking lot."

"Feel better."

I put my phone on the nightstand and buried myself in pillows. All of the debaters had departed the motel, leaving it silent except for intermittent footsteps. The wolf in a framed picture on the wall was staring at me. If the wolf had been there, I don't think it would have been interested in eating me. I wouldn't have provided any meat.

The Anorexia God enjoyed my anguish. "You're useless. What value do you add to this world?"

"You're absolutely correct."

"Look at you. You're pathetic. You're nothing. All you have is your anorexia. There isn't anything else to be proud of."

"I don't have a rebuttal."

No counter-voice emerged to temper the Anorexia God's zealous hatred of its subject. Nothing balanced the self-hatred. Nobody told me just to breathe. I was hyperventilating in the prison of my emptiness. My head was pounding from the convulsions that came with a lack of sleep and nutrition. The unprovoked, unrelenting, inescapable sadness distorted all shapes and color. The room was a kaleidoscope.

"You must not disregard how inept you are. Why are you alive?" the Anorexia God said. "What the hell are you even doing here?"

"I'm not sure." My skin felt like an uncomfortable shirt that I wanted to rip off.

"Well, I'm sure you are nothing, nothing," the Anorexia God said.

"What about last night with Katherine and Adam? They liked me."

"Yeah, that was one night. Don't expect that to last.

Good things won't last for you. They can't. You'll screw it up. I can promise you that, Jake. You screw everything up."

"I hope I can avoid a screwup."

"Hopes and expectations are distinct."

I lifted the television's remote control off the floor and smashed it against the nightstand. The black plastic exploded into hundreds of pieces that scattered across the soiled carpet. I was horrified at my trajectory from uncontaminated newborn to misery weeping in a dreary motel room. The universe seemed sardonic.

I wondered how I could have gone from falling asleep so happy to waking in turmoil. I reminded myself that sometimes highs of such happiness distracted me from my true state of misery. Behind every one of my smiles was a darkness that I didn't show the world. Once in a while, I'd temporarily forget what was hurting me. However, when the sweetness was gone, everything would become worse than it was before the relief. I'd remember, *Oh shit, I'm in pain. The escape wasn't real.* I couldn't flee my brain unless I fled my existence.

I considered that option before concluding that I didn't want to be found in a bed full of other people's ejaculate. That wouldn't have been dying with dignity. It would have been a wretched place to discover my body.

Shivering, I pulled the sheets over my head and tried to breathe. I couldn't slow my frantic heartbeat.

I wasn't sure whether I wanted to live. Maybe the best way to take control of my life was to determine how it ended. My black fake-leather belt was begging to wrap itself around my throat. It could have made everything stop.

"It will end very soon," the Anorexia God said. "I promise it will stop very soon. We are going to fix this."

"Isn't now the right time?"

"No, give the anorexia more of a chance. Don't go yet. You still have a little bit left to do here."

The divine voice in my head appeared to have moderated.

The metal rod in the gaping closet invited me to hang out, flirtatiously hinting that it had supported men three times my size before. I pushed myself off of the mattress and stepped into the tight storage space.

I left the closet and walked toward a mirror that was attached to a dresser. In front of a foggy mirror, I stripped down to my boxer shorts. This time, I didn't notice the bony body. Despair had replaced thoughts about weight loss and focused me on creating a new kind of palliative care.

"This lifestyle may kill you one day," the Anorexia God said. "Nonetheless, your goal should be to see the eating disorder through for as long as you can. It's too early for death. You can't give up on the anorexia. It's going to help. It's going to make everything better."

"You are right."

"Be a little patient. I've kept you on track this long."

I was as nauseated as I would have been if I'd smelled another person's puke. As the vomit moved toward my mouth, I sprinted to the bathroom, opened the toilet lid, dropped to my knees, and puked blood into the bowl for more than ten minutes. Everything in the room was drifting as if it were in space.

I tiptoed back to the closet and fell asleep underneath the hanging rod.

3:30 p.m.

My ringing cell phone awakened me. WuDi had texted me an update on the tournament's status: "Awards are about to start."

I packed my bag, threw up once more, brushed my teeth multiple times, and left an eighty-five-dollar tip for the maid because I regretted the mess I was too exhausted to clean.

The clerk at the front desk, where I was going to pay for the extended checkout, was Easy-Bake-Oven-level high. He was eating ketchup chips and watching *Teletubbies* on a tiny low-resolution television. Or as Jerry Falwell would have said, Tinky-Winky was indoctrinating the clerk into a subversive gay counterculture.

"Checking out?" he said as weed oozed from his breath.

"Yes, room 608, and I also damaged a remote control. So I'd like to pay for that too. You could also send me a bill for it." Beneath the two layers of sweatpants, my knees were trembling.

"Dude, you guys already checked out, man."

"But I got an extended checkout, and the previous clerk told me I'd pay when I came down."

"Nah, man. We're cool. Nobody was checking in anyway."

"I want to pay. What about the remote control?"

"It's cool. It's just a cheap little thing. It's no big deal, homie. Don't worry about it."

"Please, sir, I want to pay. Let me pay."

"We're square. S'all good."

"I need to pay. I broke the remote control. I stayed in your room after the checkout time. I have to pay for what I do—for what I did."

He giggled. "I've never seen someone so desperate to pay. Don't worry about it, dude. Have a great day."

I was infuriated. Paying for the broken remote control would have been a small gesture to compensate people for damage I had caused. My spiral was hurting those who loved me, yet I didn't know how to pay for the destruction I was causing. I viewed that interaction with the clerk as a metaphor for my inability to assume responsibility for my actions.

"Actually, I forgot something in the room. Could I go grab it?" I said to the clerk.

He handed me back the key.

I needed a couple of minutes to process the exchange with the clerk. Why would he not allow me to pay?

I jumped back into the bed and reburied myself in the sheets, under which I screamed and cried for five minutes.

"I need to pay. I have to pay. I have to," I said to the Anorexia God.

"That clerk controlled you in the situation. You lost. It's over. You lost."

I was hyperventilating. "I should go back and put money down on the table."

"Why? He'd probably spend it on potato chips and a collector's edition DVD of *My Little Pony*. Face it, Jake. You lost."

I took five deep breaths, exited the room, stepped into the mild Waterloo air, and embarked on the draining ten-minute walk to the main campus. Although the world felt like a spinning desk globe, I found the car that would take me back to Kingston.

"Where have you been all day?" Katherine asked.

"I was really tired, so I rested and worked on an essay I have to submit tomorrow," I said with a nervous smile. "Hey yo, do you think that if somebody's spouse had a terminal illness, it would be appropriate to ask the dying person to make a cast of his or her genitals for future use, or would that be way too gutty?"

"Wha? How am I even supposed to answer that? That's so wrong."

"Would you do that for your spouse, Katherine? It's okay. I won't judge you."

My pain was invisible, hidden behind comical camouflage and erased tears.

"I have an idea for a Viagra commercial. A guy with a long white beard is standing by the sea. He pops a blue pill, his shaft rises, and the sea parts. 'Viagra: talk to your doctor today.'"

Everyone in the car laughed. My mind wouldn't let me smile.

CHAPTER 22

Mauling the Past

Home Alone was on. It was a stormy February night in Kingston, and I was shivering inside my heated apartment. Sprawled across the couch and wrapped in five blankets, I fixated on the screen. I forbade my mind from relaxing. I've always loved *Home Alone*, but I wasn't watching the movie for its cinematic brilliance. Rather, it transported me into the past, the glory days that the present had hostilely taken over. I shut my eyes, listened to the film's sounds, and gave my brain the freedom to take me to the mental state in which I had first experienced the scenes.

I was tucked into my parents' bed, eating animal crackers. Dad was annoyed that Mom had permitted me to watch the movie well beyond my bedtime.

"Ell," he said while he lifted his head from underneath a fortress of pillows, "it's eight thirty. It's a school night. These bedtimes are getting absolutely ridiculous—totally out of control."

"Oh, Sam, were you never young?" she snapped. "The kids are not two years old anymore. They will be fine. Go to bed. You're always grumpy after your first nap of the evening."

Dad reburied his head in his pillows.

I had long finished the animal crackers. Mom was working on a crossword puzzle and glancing at the movie to estimate its remaining duration. Every time she looked up from the newspaper, I was nervous she was going to tell me it was time for bed. But she allowed me to finish watching the film.

The images from that night in my parents' bedroom filled my head. When I closed my eyes, I could feel Mom and Dad's cold purple-and-white sheets. I could see the closed white blackout blinds, the clunky standard-definition television, and Mom's cluttered makeup counter. I could taste the crunchy and sweet animal crackers. I could smell Mom's microwaved Orville Redenbacher popcorn. She licked the butter and salt from the inside of the bag.

I couldn't hang on to anything, but I could feel it. When I touched my bearded face, it felt smooth. My legs didn't have hair. I was missing two of my front upper teeth. My voice was high-pitched and youthful.

I was really there, suspended back in time and gliding to the rhythm of a thousand memories past. Resurrecting moments once deceased liberated me from the prison inside my mind. My body could relax and unclench. I could breathe free breaths, see free sights, and hear free sounds. The trance was like riding a bike for the first time, the trailing winds reminding me that I could pedal toward infinite yesterdays.

I was home.

My focus alternated between the action on the screen and the memories in my head. The latter alleviated the physical discomfort that accompanied my anorexia. It distracted me from my sore back, throbbing head, and heavy face. I floated through the past as if it had zero gravity.

I opened my eyes as the soundtrack to the closing credits played. The memories gave way to the present. I'd returned to the solitary confinement where I thought I might soon die. Was life worth living when happiness depended on keeping your eyes closed? What was the meaning of an existence in which your only genuine smile came from your mind's ability to turn off reality? Would the illusion end? Would the past become a drug from which I could no longer get high?

I was terrified I'd one day lose the capacity to relive the past, so I spent the next twelve hours rewatching childhood classics and listening to songs that produced portraits of old haunts. I fanatically reminisced, losing myself in the sights and sounds of soothingly painful nostalgia.

With *Matilda* playing in the background, I propped my feet up on two gray cushions and began to suck my left thumb as I had when I was a child. The digit felt as if it were shrinking into its youthful form. I was a child again. I was home again.

Such fanatical reminiscence was one of my anorexic rituals. It was meditative yet frightening. On the one hand, it allowed me to re-create the past. The reflective states cornered my existential nothingness and made me forget about the sources of my sadness. My brain selectively chose memories, neglecting the demons that had crawled around my thoughts in those years. I'd awaken from trances terrified that they were the sole mechanism through which I could feel positive emotions. The pain rushed back down my spine when I returned from the dreams. The most upsetting thought was the prospect that the images would never return. Would my senses always be so connected to the past?

I awoke at four o'clock in the morning on the second Sunday of February. *Rookie of the Year* flickered on the television screen. My teeth chattered to a subtle beat, as the four sweaters and three blankets in which I'd slept couldn't keep me warm. When I sat up to fetch another source of heat, nausea flung my body back and forth like a corpse dangling from a rope. Blood flew from my mouth like water from a waterfall and stained my white T-shirt. The rapid stream of liquids burned, scratched, and pinched my throat. I was choking on my brain.

I ran to the bathroom and knelt in front of the toilet. My protruding knees ached when they met the frigid bathroom floor. My neck was too bony to support my head, which dangled over the toilet like a semi-decapitated failure. If I'd fallen in the forest and everyone had been around to hear it, would I have made a sound?

My insides felt empty, principally because I hadn't eaten in three days, but my mouth ejected fluids, and my face submerged itself in the toilet bowl. Toilet water dripped from my almost nonexistent chin. A respite followed this unintentional purging. Then the spasms restarted. My temples smashed against the plastic seat, and blood sprayed against the base of the dual bathtub-shower, a detail that I didn't give the new tenants who moved into my apartment after I left. When the bathroom resembled a forensic scientist's playground, my dizziness worsened, and my vision became akin to a cruel hoax. The room's contents spun without any pattern. I called their motions an anorexic's Picasso.

After the bloody vomit stopped flowing about thirty-five minutes into the attack, I labored back to my bed. At first, I clutched the bathroom's counter and used it to help myself stand. I fell four times yet eventually summoned enough energy to lift myself. However, my shaking lower half and buckling knees collapsed. I landed in an almost splits position. I tried to lift myself again, competing with my wobbling thinner-than-kindling legs. Then I put my back down on the pinkish tiles, where I could not get comfortable. My unprotected bones would not let me cushion myself. Almost anything that touched me hurt, so I sought a return to the bed—my haven, my shelter, my heaven.

I started crawling toward my bedroom, but my aching body forced me to break every thirty seconds. The carpet burned through the two pairs of sweatpants I was wearing. I was panting like a Great Dane in the heat of a desert summer and was drooling without a cause. My toothpick arms trembled until they crumpled, and my face again hit the ground. I rolled over onto my back and lifted my arms to align my biceps with my shoulders, reaffirming that becoming a physical specimen was an arduous process. Annexing the utmost corporeal and mental control involved rigorous, time-consuming training. Finding the anorexia Tao was a quest. I flexed my arms and grunted, indicating the difficulty of such minimal physical exertion. "Looking much better," I told myself as I inspected each muscle.

I imagined slight muscle growth but was disappointed with the fat that continued to underscore my failures as a human being. My chin was still not the singular entity that it should have been. I lifted my sweaters to see a stomach and pelvis that were not even. My fingers were still a little chubby. My thighs remained chunky.

I challenged myself to fast for five days. I would accept a few sips of water but restrict any caloric consumption. This plan to shrink my body size and increase my muscle mass infused me with an optimism that motivated me to retry walking back to the overseas bed. I rolled onto my belly and stretched out my arms. When the floor pierced through my jutting ribcage, I aimed to use my elbows, which I pushed into the ground, to lift my upper body. Like a hunted corpse, I crashed against the carpet.

I wrapped myself in the old blue blanket that lay curled beside me. The lights began flickering, and the room spun counterclockwise. The movie's dialogue blended with the street noise.

I closed my eyes and tried to relive the moment when I'd first seen that movie, but my memory was blank. Was this it? Was this the time when I would become permanently imprisoned in the present?

"Jake!" a faraway voice shouted.

I couldn't identify the speaker, but she sounded familiar.

"Jake!" the person called again. "Jake, my son. My gorgeous boy."

It was Mom. I wasn't sure what was happening. Was I in the hospital? Was Mom really there? Was she watching me die?

"How could you do this to yourself?" she asked. "Look at you. You're killing yourself. You're going to kill us—your family. You need to start eating."

"No, thanks," I said. "I'm not hungry, and I eat enough. But you can't overeat if you want a frame like I'm building. Besides, I had a huge lunch today."

"You're not going to build any muscle this way. Everything you worked for at the gym—money down the drain. Why did you even go, my son?"

Mom had never before referred to me as "my son," so such a shift had the creepy aura of a deathbed chant or a hackneyed scene in which a poor bastard's family and friends say goodbye while a white light overpowers the party.

A small opening by the window allowed me to see Mom. She was standing across the street from my ninth-floor apartment and in front of a bar.

"Mom," I said, "do you have any avocado salad?"

"I don't serve my avocado salad to dead people. You are not alive right now. Am I supposed to open your mouth and feed the avocados to your corpse? Come on."

Her tone switched from stern to mournful.

"Wake up, my son. It's too early to sleep. You're too young to need this much sleep. Wake up, Jake. My son, please wake up. Oh my God." A gray cardigan absorbed her abundant tears.

"Mom, I have an essay due tomorrow."

"I'm sure you have finished it. You always finished your assignments really early. You were so talented, Jake. You didn't even know. You were brilliant."

"Sure, Mom."

"When did you write it?"

"Three weeks ago."

"I don't care about your essay. But I have a big surprise for you."

Mom appeared. She was standing in front of me.

"What's this surprise—that you are here right now?"

"Don't worry, my son. There's more."

She clapped her hands six times. Dad, Maddie, Bubby Pearl, Zaidy Jerry, Zaidy Paul, and Nana Sheila were all sitting on the couch to my left, each dressed in a plain black robe.

"Are you ready?" she asked them in the tone of a choreographer or a film director.

All seven of them rubbed their faces with open palms.

"Perfect," Mom told them.

I was puzzled.

"Don't worry," Mom said. "This is just the beginning. On the count of three, guys? One. Two. Three. Go."

They clawed at their eyes until all of their eyeballs

crashed against my chest and landed on my face. I was bright red with their blood.

"We can't watch you anymore," Mom said. "I can't see you like this. Come here, Molly."

Molly licked the blood off of me and then ate each of their eyeballs individually. Mom encouraged the feast.

"Good girl. You're such a good little doggy."

I woke up on the carpet, which my sweat had stained.

CHAPTER 23

Ommm

My classmates were discussing the merits of spiritual healing.

"I have a spiritual guru I swear by," a female student told the class. "I once had an eating disorder, and he took the pain away. All I wanted was control, control, control, and I learned about allowing myself to kind of succumb to the universe, ya know? It was really liberating. Honestly."

While I was skeptical of the anecdote's veracity, I wanted to ask her about this guru. What had this person said that helped her overcome a mental state that resembled mine? But I was too scared to approach the student, as I couldn't admit I would consider betraying my intellectual status by soliciting such pseudoscientific assistance.

Still, I felt hopeless enough to book an appointment with a healing guru I found in the online classifieds. I didn't believe his method would work, yet I wanted to freeze some of my pain.

Immediately after walking through the beaded entrance of the guru's townhouse, I surmised that he was more likely to offer me weed or peyote than to cure me. A tan and tall Caucasian man, the guru was wearing white cotton pants, an oversized white cotton long-sleeved T-shirt, and brown wooden sandals. He ran his fingers through his long black hair, which could have qualified him to portray any male biblical character onstage.

"Hi. My naaame is Jonath-one," he said in a hushed tone that a heavy dose of narcotics must have produced. "You must be Travis."

I'd lied about my name.

"Yes. And sorry, but you said your name was Jonathan, right?"

"No, it's actually Jonath-one—like the number one. As in we are all one," he drawled. "Now, before we begin, I will just let you knooow that I take cash, Visa, Mastercard, American Express, and debit carrrd."

"Ah, okay, I would have thought that love was your currency. What's the exchange rate between love and the American dollar nowadays? I need to know before I go to the bank to buy some love."

"Ha. I could tell that you have a sense of humor. That's very good—very gooood indeed. We need to laugh. It's good for our souls. It's part of the huuuman energy. Positive energy, my beautiful friend. Just keep everything wonderful and hummm along to the rhythm of the world's glorious enerrrgy. Life is a gift."

"Yes, I like to laugh. I have to ask. Are you related to Donny Osmond? Because if you put on a technicolor dreamcoat, you could totally pass as his version of Joseph."

"Nooo, I'm afraid I'm not familiar with the reference there. But this fellow sounds wonderrrful. Please follow meee."

Jonath-one led me down the hallway to a black room that contained a single-sized cot with a white blanket.

"I looove the contrast of colors in this room," he said. "The walls, the hardwood—everything is blaaack. It's so serene. And then the bed is white. It's like you are surrounded by darkness, and then there's this little bed. That is you, my beautiful friend, and it's white—lightness in the middle of darkness. The world may be dark, but you can still be the light. You neeed to be light."

"That sounds pretty racist to me."

"You are verrrry funny. That's good. That's sooo good. Your soul is sooo blessed. We are all so blessed. Mmm."

"Well, you set me up for that joke."

"All right, my beautiful friend. Please hop on the bed, lie on your back, and clooose your splendid eyes. Let everything fall away. Be peaceful, peaceful, peeeaceful."

I obeyed his instruction.

"Would you mind if I put on a bit of music? The soul needs music, my beautiful friend."

"Go ahead, good sir."

The trance mix that began playing gave the space an ice-pick-murder kind of vibe. "Now, I want you to turrrn off everything. Turn off the world. Don't think about a single thiiing. Love. Love. Love. Looove. Caress your forehead with your deep breaths. In and out. Okay, my beeeautiful friend?"

"I understand."

I fixated on the possibility of this guru murdering me. Was his plan to have me close my eyes and then—*boom*—stick some sort of healing dagger through my heart? Would his defense team argue that my mind was already off when he killed me?

"Now, I want you to take a biiig breath in and then a huuuge, massive, ginormous breath out."

Reluctantly, I followed his command.

"Wonderrrful. Keep your eyes closed. I'm going to start sending my energy throoough you." He rubbed my forehead with his left hand and the front of my face with his right hand. "The energy should come right through me into you just as light passes through a bulb, my beautiful friend."

I continued thinking about whether he was going to murder me.

Skipping my two secret yogis and my giver of life, he moved his palms across every accessible part of my body. At one point, he heard my stomach growl.

"Now I sense that you are hungry."

"Yes, I am anorexic."

"I knooow. I could tell by the energy that I was getting from your upper forehead and the tension in your left calf."

"Oh, you mean the emaciation and my telling you I was anorexic weren't what did it for you? Huh. You must be psychic. I'm very impressed." I recognized that I was emaciated.

"Nooo, I felt it in your energy," Jonath-one said. "Nooow, I want you to keep your eyes shut, please. Just shut off your miiind. Remove it from the world, and let yourself wander in space."

My brain was alternating between thoughts of discussions about whether an anorexic Jewish groom would have enough strength to break a glass and whether this guru ever collected his pubic hair in a bag to use it for magical healing practices.

"Let time just disappear into the rhythmically beautiful horizon. Let your *citta* rest, my beautiful friend. Let everything go away. Ommm."

I sat up and opened my eyes. "Okay, I apologize in advance for my foul language, but what the fuck did any of that mean?"

"I'm sensing some negative energy," he said as if he were a Furby that refused to shut up. "Be positive. We need positivity."

"Or my cash. I'm paying a hundred dollars for this session, and we haven't even gotten to the anorexia and depression part."

"Of courrrse we're getting there. Don't worry, my beautiful friend. You have to let me help you through my enerrrgy, my beautiful friend."

"Beautiful friend" had become an insult.

"Okay, I will give it another shot." I lay back on the apparently enchanted bed in the dark room. Jonath-one grazed my shoulder blades and began chanting.

"Ommm. Ommm. Ommm."

My spiritual healer briefly left the room and then returned with a harmonium, a keyboard instrument that generates sound through metal reeds, and muted the Buddhist trance. "Keep your eyes clooosed, my beautiful friend."

Jonath-one chanted and played an unrecognizable, flat melody that I mentally transformed into "YMCA."

The music ceased.

"Open your eyes, my beautiful friend."

Was my reunification with sight supposed to bring newfound clarity?

"Nooow, my beautiful friend, I can feel that something has been hurting you, and I know that you're not eating. Nourishment is a way to fill the body with the energy that it needs to be that beautiful and wonderful vessel that interacts with the rest of the uuuniverse.

"You have to eeeat. Food is what nourishes your soul and brings out the beauty in life. There can be days when you fast to bring your mind and body closer together. But you must eat mooore than you are eating now. Okay, my beautiful friend? That is really, really what you need to do. Just make the body stay beautiful inside and out."

"It's that easy?"

"You need to reach deeep down into your soul to find the beeeautiful, holy energy. Ommm."

The guru lit a scented candle, muttered a few words that might have been a prayer under his breath, and collected his cash. "I'm sorry. I don't have a receeeipt for you."

No shit. "Really? That's a shame, as I was going to put this visit through my insurance."

"Goodbye, my beautiful friend. Be loving. Keeep your spirit alive. Maybe I will see you sooon."

I stepped back into a world that seemed more hopeless than it had when I'd walked through those beads. I was disgusted with myself. Investing time and money in quackery showed me how desperate I was to feel better about myself. I'd suspended my critical-thinking capacity, the quality I was most proud of, because I was so frantic for answers.

Looking back on the experience now, I can see hope in it. I was searching in the wrong places for answers, but at least I was searching. That I took that quest to a place I would have shunned in any other scenario exemplified how much I sought salvation.

CHAPTER 24

Heretic

It was three thirty in the morning in late March, and I was texting my mother. The central benefit of her menopausal hot flashes was that they kept her awake at night, giving me somebody to speak to as I sat alone in the darkness of my one-bedroom apartment.

"I miss home. I don't really have that many friends here," I wrote.

"The year is almost over. End it on a good note."

"I'm trying. There are some days when I can't get out of bed, when my sheets seem like the best place to be. I don't know why I'm so sad all the time. I just am. I can't help it. It's like a disease."

"What do you want me to do?" she asked. "Do you think you need to come home? I could come out there too."

I ignored that option. As an eighteen-year-old guy, the last thing I wanted was my mommy to move in with me.

"No, you're right. I should definitely finish my first year here and then maybe transfer to the University of Toronto so that I could live at home. That may be better."

I didn't expect to live that long.

"Do you need me to come out and stay there for a few days?"

I would have loved the company but didn't want to inconvenience Mom.

"No, no. That would be ridiculous. I'm in classes and meetings all day. You'd be bored, and I can manage. I'm having a shitty time right now."

"I worry about you."

"Hey, people always requested that I fast for Yom Kippur. Right now, I guess I am just doing an extended version of atonement."

"Not funny at all."

"I'm coming in for the weekend tomorrow. I haven't been back in like a month."

"That's so nice. Did you get a train ticket?"

"No, I'm hitchhiking with a nice trucker named Todd. He told me I would have to blow him once (max twice) for a ride. He has a weird thing for skinny eighteen-year-old men. Who knew that was a thing?"

"Sounds like a pretty good deal to me. Very gutty."

I shut off my phone. The room was dark and silent. My world felt as empty as my stomach. Existence lost its mystery. I'd always been sad, yet the sources of my sadness once had been identifiable and ever changing. During my ano years, I couldn't point to one origin and instead lived under an almost never-fading sense of doom. I viewed happiness as momentary absences of sadness, a feeling to embrace while knowing it was going to give way to an abyss.

I missed my parents, but I was nervous about going home. Their threat perception was too shrill and obsessive. How could I have expected anything different? I was killing myself with an illness that seemed to have such an easy solution. "Just eat," they'd tell me. They were correct. If I'd consumed even 50 percent of a healthy diet, I wouldn't have looked like a walking skeleton with a bit of skin as gift wrap. They were right to be terrified at the realistic prospect of my death. In September, I had pondered whether I was going to live to see my nineteenth birthday. Since I'd seen them in late January, however, I had lost another fifteen pounds, shrinking to a point that would no doubt make their sleepless nights even more restless and their graying hair a little grayer.

"Okay," I texted Mom a few minutes before I left my apartment for the train station. "If I am going to come home, you have to promise that you and Dad will not say a single thing about my weight. Otherwise, I'm not going to get on the train and will stay here for the weekend. I know you're worried. I appreciate that. You need to know that I am working through things, and screaming about it will not be helpful. I promise you that hysteria won't do anything productive. That's what my therapist has been telling me."

I was lying, as I hadn't seen my therapist in a while. *Yeah, I'm killing my insides and dying in front of you, but you should shut your mouths about it.*

Their faces crinkled when they saw me emerge from Union Station, struggling to keep a backpack on my bony shoulders and drowning in a heavy winter coat that had become about seventeen thousand sizes too large. A jacket and jeans, not a human, were walking toward them. As soon as I opened the door to Mom's black SUV, I knew they were not going to fulfill their promise to avoid yelling about my condition.

"Holy shit, Jake," Dad said as he pulled away from the curb. "How did you even get to the car with the wind out today?"

"You're worse than when we left you there," Mom added. "Oh my God. What are you doing to yourself? What has happened?"

"I guess you could call it my Ramadan," I said.

"No, this is not a joke at all anymore," Mom said, her voice alternating between trembling and assertiveness. "This is serious. How much more weight have you lost? I mean, look at you. Oh my God. I don't even know what there is to say right now."

"I haven't lost weight. Don't overreact. They weighed me at the hospital and, in fact, found that I had gained half a pound. I know that half a pound does not mean anything at all. Within a day, weight fluctuates between one or two pounds, but I have been steady for the semester."

"That's a load of shit," Mom said, calling me on my obvious lie. "There is no way you haven't lost weight. Just look at you. You can barely keep your head up. It's like your head is going to fall off your neck. Your body is just going to crumple into nothing. What am I supposed to do? What do I say? Do you want to look like an anorexic? Do you think that looks good at all? You're too smart to be doing this to yourself. You get all perfect grades, yet you're being too stupid to realize that you're killing yourself. Absolutely killing yourself. How could you let yourself go like this? Do you not care? Do you think it's a joke?"

"This is why I was hesitant about coming home at all. I just wanted a nice weekend away from school to see everyone, not to listen to lectures about my eating habits."

"I know you were hesitant, but, Jake, come on," Mom said. "You can't expect me to stand idly by and say, 'Okay, okay, you can just go off and do this to yourself.' What kind of parent would that make me? I can't not say anything. It's not fair to expect me not to give a shit."

Mom uses double negatives when she's upset.

"I'm not saying that you can't care or can't be worried—not at all," I said. "I don't think you have anything to worry about, and you are blowing all of this way, way out of proportion. You have a tendency to freak about things that don't require panic. If I get a little cold or even sneeze once, you think I'm dying. 'Is that a cough I'm hearing? It doesn't matter that the cough came from choking on a Popsicle. You have to go see the doctor.' That's how you think about things, Mom. You see everything through a terrified motherly perspective. You need to be calm and realize that not everything is life threa—"

"If you really believe there's nothing wrong with you, then you're really in deep trouble, Jake. You can't not see it. I refuse to believe that."

"You don't understand. I'm eating healthy. I still have fat on my stomach. You can't even see my abs. I'm really not that skinny."

"You sound like an anorexic. Are you in denial?"

"I'm not anorexic."

"How do you not see how skinny and unhealthy you look? All of my friends see pictures of you and think, *Oh my God*. Do you want to look like that? It doesn't look nice."

"Which friends?"

"All of them."

"Name one."

She listed almost ten of her friends who had allegedly commented on my emaciation, which they had seen through images on social media.

"You're probably making that up."

"Okay, ask them. Go right ahead."

Mom put her head in her hands.

That night's argument continued until the car pulled into our driveway, but it would last for the remainder of the weekend. My parents repeated the same lines and questions as if they were searching for a definitive answer, something to explain the physical and mental decay unfolding under their powerless watch. Home was like a cheap hotel, a place where I could feel neither settled nor comfortable. I had difficulty falling asleep in my bed.

Mom knocked on my door the next afternoon. My door was closed, and I hadn't left my room. I told her she could come in.

"Are you going to be able to go for dinner tonight?" Mom asked, referring to our plans scheduled for that evening.

"Yeah, why wouldn't I be able to go for dinner?"

"Look at you. You've been in bed all day. You can't lift your head off the pillow."

"I'm just tired. I was working on a couple of essays really late last night."

I was lying again, as the real source of my exhaustion was a mixture of depression and malnutrition.

"Don't lie to me. This is not being tired from doing homework. You've done homework all of your life and stayed up late many times before. It's really easy to see that this is different."

"You can believe that if you want, but it's not true. Every time I sleep during the day or admit that I'm tired, you think the entire world is crumbling right before you."

"Oh, come on, Jake. I am a lot swifter than you give me credit for. I wasn't born yesterday. I know you like a book."

"Well, then I guess you don't know books very well."

"What have you eaten today?"

"While you were gone, I had the pasta that you made me."

I'd fed the noodles to Molly.

"I don't believe you."

"Check the fridge."

"That doesn't necessarily mean you ate them. You could have given them to the dog. I mean, you still can't even get out of bed."

"You're just wrong. Watch this. I can easily stand up and be active. I'll take the pooch out for a walk—no problem. Let's go, Molly!" I called. "Do you want to go for a walk?"

As Molly sprang from her corner of the room, I slowly propelled my body from the bed, rising gingerly to avoid snapping myself in two. Everything hurt. My bones, muscles, and joints were furious that my brain was at once destroying them and making them work. They were not going to allow me to walk Molly for more than a few minutes, but I needed to show my mother that I was healthy and full of energy. After walking a block down the familiar sidewalk, I was as exhausted as a couch potato would have been after having sex with an Olympic gymnast.

I turned the corner and sat on the curb, where I passed forty minutes texting Uncle Steve about the struggling Toronto Maple Leafs hockey team. "Sorry to disappoint you, Molly," I said to her. "This is as far as we are going today."

She looked back at me as if to say, "It's a nice day. Walk me, you pussy."

Molly tilted her head to the right and then lay down on the sidewalk.

Sitting underneath the prespring sunshine, I wondered whether potential onlookers would have mistaken me for the twigs that had emerged from underneath the snow.

That night's dinner at one of the finest restaurants in the city made me anxious. At home, I could be furtive and dishonest about my eating habits. Even if my parents didn't believe I had eaten, I could claim they were incorrect and argue about facts rather than empirical evidence. A restaurant presented a frightening obstacle, for Mom and Dad could observe every bite or lack thereof. I considered faking an illness, but such a strategy would have elicited calls that my lack of nutrition had made me sick.

"I'm not very hungry tonight," I told them at the restaurant. "I think I'll just have a salad."

"Oh no you will not," Dad said. "Absolutely not."

"No, really, I had a big lunch."

"What did you have—a large banana? Wowee, that's a big lunch."

"You need to stop. I'm eating. Everything is fine. I appreciate the concern, but it's not warranted here."

"Bullshit."

Dad wouldn't let me order for myself.

"He will start with the lentil soup, and as an entrée, he'll go with the brown rice penne in a tomato sauce with sautéed mushrooms, asparagus, and broccoli on the side," Dad informed the server.

"No, Dad, that's way too much food for me."

"Eat what you can. You have to eat."

Before the appetizer, the server brought a small plate of bruschetta to the table.

"Have a piece, Jake," Dad said.

"I'm all right. You all enjoy."

"It won't kill you to have a piece." Mom sighed.

"Leave him alone," Maddie said, lifting her eyes from her phone. "If he wants to eat, he'll eat. Stop freaking out."

"Mind your business," Mom said.

"Have the bruschetta," Dad continued.

I ate a piece because I wanted to mitigate the tension. With each bite, I estimated the calories that my body was absorbing. I continually grabbed my minimal belly fat to examine the damage of this indulgence.

"Have one more," Dad said, pointing to the last remaining piece on the plate.

"No, no. I have soup coming and then pasta with all those veggies. And I had a big lunch. You have the last piece."

"Just eat it. Live a little. It won't kill you."

"It will keep me from finishing my dinner."

"Come on. Enjoy it. Eat."

Again, I surrendered. The Anorexia God was screaming at me.

"Are you kidding? That's probably more than two hundred calories, more than you're supposed to have in one serving. You also have more food coming soon. This is a disaster. You're going to get fat tonight. Wait until you look in the mirror."

"What am I supposed to do?" I said, continuing the conversation with the voice in my head. "I'm definitely not going to run to the bathroom to throw up. I couldn't do that. It grosses me out."

"Yeah. Besides, puking is not part of our faith. You need to be tough and tell them that you're full from the bruschetta. Remind them of your big lunch. Make up more lies. They are going to whine and moan. You'll have to be strong and get through it for yourself—for us. Okay?"

"I'm going to try. The lentil soup is probably small and not that high in calories. There is no way I can avoid eating that, so I'll misbehave a little tonight. As soon as they all fall asleep, I'll jump rope in the basement."

"Skip the lentil soup too."

"I can't do that."

The soup should have tasted delicious, but it was like eating poison.

"What the hell is wrong with you?" the Anorexia God said. "A good weight clearly doesn't mean anything to you. You want to lose control."

"I didn't have much of a choice."

"Sure you did. I am your father."

"Don't worry. I will take one bite of the pasta and tell them I am too full to eat it, so they should pack it up. I'll let my dad have it tomorrow."

After one taste of the pasta, I claimed I couldn't eat any more. "I am so full. Maybe we could wrap it up, and I'll eat it tomorrow."

"Attaboy," the Anorexia God said.

"You could eat it, Jake," Dad said.

I took another bite.

"Stop. Stop. Stop," the Anorexia God said.

"See? There you go. Enjoy it. Relax. Lighten up," Dad said.

"Please stop. What has gotten into you, Jake?"

"It must be nice to eat normal food for once," Mom said.

"Ignore your mother," the Anorexia God said. "Do not pay attention to the happiness that your eating is bringing your parents. Tell them you're full. Stop now."

I took more bites.

"Have some mushrooms," Dad said.

"Stop. Please."

"And some asparagus."

"Don't do it. You need to quit before you totally lose control."

"Here is a little broccoli to add to the pasta."

"Look how much oil is on that broccoli. Keep it away from your mouth."

The pasta and sautéed vegetables were soon gone, yet they would torment me for the rest of the week. I was pinching what I believed was new belly flab and hoping it would recede with the digestion process.

"You probably gained like five pounds tonight," God said. "Shame on you, Jake. You're a disgrace."

I waited until the house was quiet before tiptoeing down the stairs to the basement gym, where I ran on the spot until the dizziness was unbearable. I had to burn off some of the excess calories that had poisoned me.

The analysts on the radio broadcast I was listening to were debating whether Donald Trump could win any states in a Republican primary. Normally, I would have carefully listened to such a discussion, yet I was fixated on my earlier transgressions. Nothing else in the world mattered. I was trapped inside the narrow and self-centered thoughts of an anorexic.

After a post-workout shower, I snuggled beside Molly in my dark bedroom and studied the sounds of my breathing. I could feel the tears falling from my eyes down to my lips and sometimes into my mouth.

"You deserve to cry," the Anorexia God said. "You really screwed up tonight. Royally."

My body was shaking, and I was short of breath. The Anorexia God interrupted all of my attempts to persuade myself that one lousy meal would not alter my anorexic project.

"Think about the number of calories in that one

meal. Let's be super conservative and estimate it around a thousand. It's probably more. You have barely eaten that much over the last few weeks, so a thousand calories could do a lot of damage. It could shock your system. It could put five pounds on you right away, even with your little workout in the basement. You want to get fat."

I was excited to return to life away from home.

Maddie heard me tiptoe to my room and followed me.

"What's going on, Jake?" she said before she sat on my bed and leaned her head against the headboard.

I lay on the carpeted floor. "I just did a little workout downstairs," I replied.

"No, what is going on in your life?"

"Things are things, you know."

"No, like, I don't know. How is Tiffany?"

"I don't know. We'll see."

"And you're not eating?"

"No."

"Why not?"

Maddie grabbed a pillow from the other side of the bed and placed her folded arms on it. She checked her phone for the first time.

"I know I should," I said. "What I'm doing isn't healthy. I get that. I get—"

"So why don't you eat?"

"The rational voice in my mind tells me that I need to eat, that this lifestyle is unhealthy, and that I have value. The problem is, that irrational voice has assumed godlike status for me. It tells me that any self-worth I have comes from the control I take over my body. I haven't figured out how to shut that voice off."

I told Maddie about the isolation I'd felt as a child, accepting that those perceptions derived mostly from cognitive distortions.

"You need to realize your value. You do great things for people. You're helpful. You're generous. You're smart. You're the best brother anybody could ask for. Think about how many people care about you. Like, if people didn't care about you this much, we wouldn't be so upset about what you're going through."

Maddie couldn't persuade me to leave the Anorexia God. I told her I'd consider what she'd said. The truth was, I wasn't going to reroute my mind.

After we spent an hour reminiscing about people of our pasts, Maddie hopped out of the bed.

"I'm always here for you," Maddie said as she left my room. "Good night."

CHAPTER 25

The Garden of Eating

Late on Sunday evening, my train arrived in Kingston, where the customary fifteen cabs lined up to greet the hundreds of arriving passengers. I opted to wait inside the station until the ratio was somewhat reasonable. Two students noticed my strategy and followed me to the rows of empty chairs in the dated lounge. We scattered ourselves, engaging in the traditional urban approach of staying far away from other human beings. After all, one of us could have had the avian flu, so pretending to play games on our phones while secretly judging one another based on the most superficial characteristics was sensible. We all knew we'd wind up sharing a taxi, yet speaking first was risky.

I put my phone in my pocket and shut my eyes to reflect upon my failure at the restaurant. I could feel the noodles, which I'd eaten more than twenty-four hours ago, expanding in my stomach. The room seemed to be getting smaller, the walls moving closer together on their way to crushing me.

"Breathe, Jake," the Anorexia God said. "We're going to get through this. Don't worry. Before we do anything, I need you to quietly get up and go to the bathroom so you can see the damage you have done. This will be a nice wake-up call about what you need to do going forward."

"I don't know that I can. I'm irrelevant. I hurt everyone around me. I'm crafting a path of destruction."

"You're not thinking right. You matter. You must not forget that control is our primary commandment. We are getting there. We haven't arrived yet. But do you not care about those around you? If you care, you'll keep being anorexic."

"Look at me. I'm a disaster. I should never have been born."

I stepped toward a mirror that hung above a rusty sink.

"Now that you are by a mirror, I want you to lift up your shirt and study your belly. Pay attention for things that may have changed in the last day or two, okay?"

"What the fuck?" I almost cried as I pinched the flab that had invaded my anorexic canvas. "It's everywhere. It's come back. What have I done? Have I ruined everything? How will I get back on track without wrecking my relationship with Mom and Dad?"

As vomit stirred in my gut and shot up to my throat, I jumped into an open stall, knelt in front of the toilet, and swerved away from a chewed piece of gum. The stream flowed from my mouth. What I first thought was pasta sauce was blood. I saw two or three slices of rhubarb, carrot fragments, and mashed cucumber, but the liquid was bright red.

"You're okay. You're okay. You're okay," the Anorexia God said as if he were a real person rubbing my perspiring back. "We're going to get through this together. You can do it. Be strong."

I wondered whether I should see a doctor because the blood might have pointed to a critical health problem. Instead, I planned to cleanse. After the fiasco with my parents, I'd allow myself nothing other than cucumbers, water, and carrots. I needed to restrain myself. I had to take control indefinitely.

I cleaned the toilet seat, on which a few drops of vomit had strayed. When I left the bathroom, one person remained in the seating area, and the row of cabs had vanished.

"Sir, I'm afraid the station is closed, so I'm going to have to ask you to leave the building," an employee with a French accent said.

For fifty minutes, I stood outside on a mild late-winter night—which was like being shirtless in the Arctic to an emaciated anorexic—until a cab picked me up and took me to my apartment.

Six Days Later

Hunger pains were becoming inescapable. I'd wake and fall asleep with a throbbing stomach and a feeling of emptiness in every part of my body. Any morsel of food was alluring.

I noticed an acrid avocado resting on the kitchen counter. The shell was softer than an obese belly, yet it looked serene. It was the answer, a panacea that could quell the incessant aches and restore a grain of clarity to the blurry vision that came with a six-day fast.

"Don't even think about it," the Anorexia God said. He could sense that temptation was challenging my anorexic orthodoxy. My almost naked counter was transforming into a Garden of Eden in which some sadistic deity had crafted lousy rules to test the limits of the subject's loyalty.

"It has been six days since I've eaten anything. Are you trying to kill me? An avocado wouldn't hurt too much," I said.

"Wouldn't hurt too much? You have to be kidding, right? There's so much fat in an avocado."

"But it's a good kind of fat. It's monounsaturated, so it increases high-density lipoprotein. It would be good for me."

"No, fat is high in calories, which means you will gain weight. Avocado is a nonstarter. Have a pickle, okay?"

"I'm sick of pickles. How many of those salty Kermit the Frog penises can I eat? It's getting ridiculous."

"Have a cucumber. Have more water. I'll even let you have a few carrots."

"Let me? You don't own me. You don't—"

"Show some respect. You're right. I don't just own you; I created you."

"The only thing you created was this emaciated monster I've become. Some creation."

"That's all you think of me?"

"I think you're a paranoid megalomaniac piece of shit."

"Remember how you felt before I arrived? How quickly you've forgotten the fat, awkward nothing. You were a lump of shit without any meaning, any purpose, or any real accomplishments."

"I had the highest average in my grade-twelve class. That was an accomplishment."

"We both know that's a bullshit achievement. Congratulations. When somebody crunched a few numbers, you had the highest one. What does that actually mean? There isn't anything existential about a percentage. Within a few minutes, everybody forgets about it."

"I remember it."

"Who cares?"

I was furious.

I sprang off the couch and took four steps before reaching the kitchen. Shivering in the heated apartment, I ripped open the avocado to reveal stringy and slimy brown flesh. The fruit's insult to the senses didn't dissuade me from devouring it without any cutlery. Letting the pit crash against the frigid linoleum floor, I ravaged the avocado with my hands and tongue. With each bite, the physical pain faded. I couldn't taste anything.

The most substantial meal I'd eaten that week disappeared in less than thirty seconds.

"Are you happy now, you moron?" the Anorexia God asked. "Look what you have done. That's at least three hundred calories, probably way more. Take off your shirt. I dare you. Look how your belly has ballooned."

"It's not going to balloon after a few hundred calories. Don't be ridiculous."

"Oh yeah? Take off your shirt, and go to the mirror. Just watch. I know exactly when it will happen, like a sunrise."

"You're being ridiculous."

"Listen to me already."

I removed four sweaters and a T-shirt before walking toward the mirror.

What I saw shocked me. I thought my eyesight must have been failing, for the filthy image that shot back at me couldn't have been real. The Anorexia God was right. My belly had expanded to at least ten times the size it had been a few hours prior. My thighs were chunky again, and the triple chin I aimed to hide in my pictures had returned. I wanted to be gazing at a stranger in the mirror, but that flabby collection of unwanted parts was really me.

"I told you. I tried to warn you." The Anorexia God laughed.

"You don't have to gloat about it."

"You're right. I'm sorry for being such a dick. Come back to me, Jake."

"I love you, and I want to be the best anorexic there is. But maybe I can't do it. Perhaps high marks are as far as I will come to accomplishing anything. I think I've failed at anorexia."

"Nonsense. You haven't failed. You just slipped up."

"No, no, I'm a failure. Why can't you see it?"

I crumpled to the carpet in front of the mirror and allowed the tears to bounce off my concave belly.

"Give it another try, Jake."

"I can't. I'm a loser. I'm a wimp." I was hyperventilating.

"Don't let this mistake get to you."

"It's not merely a little mistake. Food has become so enticing. I can't do this anymore. I'd rather die."

The Anorexia God didn't respond. Was my anorexia dead? Had it become incapable of nourishing me? Or did it not know how to respond to my condemnation?

"Are you there?"

Nothing.

"Hello?"

Nothing.

"Say something that makes me not want to end it all. Please."

Nothing.

"Please."

Nothing.

"Please."

Nothing.

"This is the last chance for me."

Nothing.

Had salvation vanished?

I hurried to the bathroom to look for the Tylenol bottle Mom had left for me when I arrived in Kingston.

The tears and returned hunger obscured the contents

of the medicine cabinet. I grabbed the first bottle I could clutch. It was shampoo.

I knew I couldn't kill myself with that. Jumping off the balcony would have been too messy and would have put people on the ground at risk. Being remembered as a smashed bottle of strained tomatoes also wasn't appealing. So I searched for the Tylenol.

After five failed attempts to find the bottle, I scurried to the kitchen and ripped a serrated knife out of the drawer. Choking its red plastic base in my frozen, sweaty right hand, I held the knife against my exposed chest. The blade grazed my few chest hairs and cooled my already cold skin. Maybe, I thought, salvation was in the knife.

My landline rang.

"Hi, Jake. It's Bubby," the voice said.

"Hello. What's going on?" I said, trying to sound as if nothing were unusual.

"Not much. I'm on the way back from a facial and sitting in traffic. Downtown is such a mess. I just wanted to check up on you and see how you're doing. I haven't spoken to you in a bit."

"You should take the subway."

"You're right, but I hate being squished in with that many people. Anyway, how are you?"

"I'm good, thanks. I just got back from a debating meeting like thirty seconds ago, so you caught me at the perfect time."

As the ordinary conversation continued, a haunting scene filled my brain: I was back at the cottage, running to the room next door and jumping into Bubby and Zaidy's bed. All three of us were excited to be with one another. I was a toddler tucked underneath the warm sheets and my grandparents' love.

"How's school?"

The words stuck in my mind.

"Are you still there?"

All sounds were clogged. I was horrified at the imminent calamity that my family was about to face.

"Jeez, this traffic is a nightmare."

"I'm sorry. I have a meeting in an hour, and I have to go make dinner."

"Okay, good to talk to you. I love you."

"I love you too."

The call's end brought me back into solitude, and I rubbed the knife against my chest again.

My neighbors were caressing other things while I was caressing the knife.

"Aaaah, Jesus Christ, you're my okapi!" she yelled.

"Oh yeah, and you're my sexy beaver."

"No. No. Not in my hair. Don't do it in my hair, please."

The noise disappeared, and I returned to finality. I counted down aloud.

"Ten. Nine. Eight. Seven. Six. Five."

My cell phone vibrated.

I let my right hand and the knife fall to my side and checked the device.

"Hey, it's Katherine. Do you want to come for dinner with WuDi and me tonight?"

"Where?"

"The Lazy Scholar in like twenty minutes?"

Why not give life one final chance? I thought. The blade wasn't going to disappear.

I dropped the knife, put on a T-shirt and a closet full of sweaters, brushed my teeth, left my apartment, and walked ten minutes through the subzero Kingston winter.

Oh, and before I left, I slipped another note under my neighbors' door:

> To my favorite lovers,
>
> Kudos for knowing what an okapi is. And I hope you have lots of shampoo.
>
> Love,
>
> A neighbor
>
> XoXo

Death could wait.

Katherine waved me over to their table.

I forced a smile and greeted them. "How are my two favorite Chinese Jews? Did you invite me here for a threesome? I'm not into that. Sorry to disappoint you."

"Oh, Jake Roth." WuDi double-tapped my head. "Jake Roth."

"We're worried about you," Katherine said. "You should have something to eat. I have lots of money left on my meal plan, so I could get you something."

"I had a big dinner."

They didn't contest this untruth.

"Katherine and I are concerned about your health, Jake. How are you doing?" WuDi said, his voice measured.

"I'm good. Can we not talk about it? You know I'm anorexic, and it's not easy, but I'm getting through it. It's not like I'm going to stab myself with a kitchen knife or anything like that. S'all good in the gutty hood, yo."

"Good. We love you, and we're here for you," WuDi said.

"I love you guys too," I replied as my eyes struggled to remain open.

I meant the sentiment, but I could not love myself; I couldn't even like myself.

"You two have been such amazing friends. Thanks for everything. I don't think you could fathom how much you two mean to me—really, you're amazing people. I'm very lucky to have you in my life."

I was wrestling with my body, trying to remain sitting up at the table but too weak to stay for more than fifteen minutes. WuDi and Katherine both hugged me and repeated a familiar refrain: "You'll get through this."

I worried that my bones would collapse in their embrace.

CHAPTER 26

The Raft That Tried to Drown Me

St. Patrick's Day 2011

The fluorescent green digits on the cable box's clock, which showed 2:02, lit the dark apartment. Everything was dead. The fluffy carpet was a trench in which scrunched pillow corpses lay. A rotting apple, with its barely recognizable green peel and exposed core, was lifeless on the kitchen counter. Dirty clothes were strewn across the floor.

Curtains secured my palace of sober insobriety from the drunkenness outside. Inebriated students who posed as Irish roamed the streets, howling and singing incomprehensibly. Smashing bottles were the percussion of piercing human voices. I don't know whether the sounds of shattering glass were real or products of hallucinations. Regardless of their origins, the noises tormented me.

An operatic tenor voice sang "Amazing Grace" in my head. The lyrics were insignificant. Such a cliché tune, which appears on too many depressing soundtracks, added normalcy to what I deemed the ultimate abnormality: terminating my existence. I believed I'd grown up to be different, but I wanted my life's potential credits to follow an unremarkable denouement. That hymn inserted something cliché into my life; it was calmingly ordinary. "Amazing grace. How sweet the sound."

I put my head down on the carpet and shut my eyes. Images rushed through my mind. Birthday celebrations, Molly sprinting, Friday night dinners, and Aunt Karrie chastising me for using inappropriate language in front of her youngest nephew zoomed in and out of my consciousness.

"Um, Jake, Aaron is way too young to learn the f-word," Aunt Karrie said, pointing her finger at me.

"What is the f-word?" I laughed.

Each picture emerged as a thumbnail but then turned into a billboard before vanishing. One memory, however, wouldn't leave.

Preschool students in oversized paper crowns formed a circle on a square rug. Jewish posters provided the room with an indisputable identity. Holiday symbols, many of which were student created, brightened a dull classroom that smelled of yellowing books. Dim lighting, dropped ceilings, and a pale paint color gave the place an industrial air. Within an hour, you could have transformed the space into an accounting office. West of the rug, parents, grandparents, caregivers, and infant siblings fixated on the students' Hanukkah performance. They sat on unpadded and narrow orange plastic chairs.

The teacher dropped to the floor as she left her padded throne for the slums that her students occupied daily.

Ms. T. was a tall, thoughtful woman with dark brown hair that rested on her shoulders. Newly formed wrinkles gave her face a taste of maturity, while the bags under her eyes resembled the light gray backdrop of a 1950s film. She appeared tired but not exhausted, aged but not old. Her clothing—a white long-sleeved top and black slacks—didn't blend with the unimpressive room.

"The next song is 'Antiochus, Why Are You So Nasty?'" Ms. T. announced to the circle. "And a one, and a two, and a three."

A camera flashed.

Most of the kids began the song on command. Others picked their noses and gazed at the hypnotic ceiling pattern. I mumbled the lyrics. The teacher peeked around the labyrinth of crowns and threw a gentle smile at me. I looked away from her as my eyes twitched. She pointed her palms to the sky and raised them gradually to indicate that she sought increased volume.

"Antiochus, why are you so nasty?" some sang.

My inarticulate singing continued. "Anacha ... hmmm ... nast. Wh-why?"

My lips stopped moving as phlegm engulfed my throat. Crying would have contradicted my newfound big-boy status, so I tried to look away from the source of potential tears.

Mom, Dad, Bubby, and Zaidy Jerry sat in the audience. I hated the fifteen feet of separation. I couldn't escape their magnetism. I needed to be with them. Twitches turned to extended blinking, and swallows became gulps. My chorus of cries commenced when the crown tumbled from my forehead and onto my face. Like a trained dog, I sprinted to the third row, jumped into my mother's lap, and buried my head in her stomach. Her maternity shirt and my juvenile skin trapped the untamed tears. I panted and sniffled. My heart beat rapidly.

"Come on, Jake," she said, rubbing my back. "We're going to go back up there."

I shook my head in her stomach, which she must have enjoyed, given that she had recently given birth to my sister. She put her hand on my chin and lifted my head.

"We're going back up there," Mom demanded. "Here we go."

She picked me up off her lap, grabbed my hand, and directed me back to the circle.

The storm's remnants still covered my face. Bloodshot eyes and flooded cheeks were downed trees and deep puddles, reminders of tranquility's fleetingness. The hammer in my head pounded to the rhythm of the class's music.

Mom walked with me to the rug. She was wearing denim overalls that hid her receding pregnancy belly. Ms. T., who had moved inward to close the circle in my absence, returned to her previous position. Mom assumed the spot I'd used before my tantrum, and I sat in her lap.

"I have a little dreidel. I made it out of clay," the class sang.

"And when it's dry and ready, then dreidel I shall play," Mom sang, joining in.

My new chair turned to me and asked that I participate. Mumblefest continued.

"Oh dreid … mmm of clay. And whe … read … Then dreid … play."

Mom winced as I used her lap as a trampoline. For two songs, she withstood my constant movement but called for a replacement.

Bubby wore a basic white long-sleeved crewneck and light blue jeans. Her dyed blonde hair, which extended to her neck, didn't move. She had a light coat of makeup on her face.

I wiggled on my new springboard until the class concluded the concert with its magnum opus, "Judah the Maccabee." Families applauded the kids and filed out. Some parents waited to hear from the teacher lies about their children being angels who were destined for greatness, yet I wouldn't let my team engage in any such dialogue. Nobody could have stolen their attention, for I protected them. I would never let go. I never wanted to let go.

The noises outside my apartment interrupted the dream.

I opened my eyes. The motion picture that had played in my head was over. Sweat poured down my cheeks and formed reservoirs in my armpits. I was the little boy on the rug again. The crown was sliding down my forehead, but this time, I had neither a place to run nor a lap to sit on. I was stuck in the circle from which salvation had disappeared.

I fanatically reminisced, idealizing the past, and mourned a life that I wanted to expire. The past was a fatality of the present.

"Shit," I muttered.

The room was doing a triple axel. My head was pounding with the increasing volume of "Amazing Grace." I started coughing. The violence of the respiratory reflexes intensified until they reached a point of all-consumption. My stomach and lungs throbbed, while the rest of my body was numb. I was sweaty but freezing.

I rolled onto my stomach and attempted to propel myself with my hands and emaciated belly. My pathetic grunts underscored the futility of the first attempt. Then I tried to lift myself onto my knees. I fell onto my back and uttered a feeble "Crap." Three days of fasting had robbed me of any strength.

I was coughing like an asthmatic cow, as my first two failures to stand on my own feet had drained any ounce of life that my body might have stored. Nonetheless, I was determined to battle my knock-knees and tender legs. On my elbows, I used every bit of energy I had left to stand on my feet.

I stumbled to the frigid bathroom, where my 112.5-pound,

five-foot-eleven body, which I mummified in four sweaters, a winter hat, two pairs of socks, a ski jacket, and winter gloves, shivered. The mirror reflected my perceived fatness. "Absolutely disgusting," I said to myself.

I crashed to my butt in front of the toilet. Would this be where they found me? Thankfully, the bowl was open, for my blurred vision made aiming my spray impossible. The coughing intensified as streams of blood met the water. The unintentional purging lasted for at least a minute. You lose track of time while puking out your insides.

When the stream stopped, red liquid covered my face. Drool flowed from my mouth. My breath reeked of emptiness. I looked like a deranged carnivore from a cheap vampire film.

I found the bottle of Tylenol on the floor behind the trash can. It must have fallen off the counter.

The pills were another shelter. They carried a comforting aura of salvation that soothed my aching body and slowed my racing brain. For the first time in months, the despair and regret faded into hope. I believed I could turn everything off. Life made sense. I was going to become a martyr for the Anorexia God. The best way to demonstrate my devotion was to give up life—definitive submission. It was a sign of both love and obedience.

My outstretched arm accidentally hit the remote control, turning on the television, which displayed *Toddlers and Tiaras*. Two mothers with thick southern accents were screaming at each other. If my depression hadn't made me want to kill myself ...

I sat up and clutched a blue pad of paper and a dull red pen that I'd buried underneath a stained dress shirt in front of my feet. My trembling hands made writing difficult, so I resigned myself to terseness. I scribbled the following:

To all those who care,

I apologize for my cowardice. You neither deserve nor are responsible for this sordid decision.

Thank you for everything.

Love,

Jake

I then answered a text message that my friend Lyndsay Lyons had sent me hours earlier.

"Hey, Jake, how are things? Are you doing all right? Text me if you need anything."

"Aw, you're so sweet for asking. I'm doing great. I've been really busy with schoolwork and debating. I can't wait for the summer. How are you? Thanks for being such an amazing friend. I'm so grateful."

I put my phone away and stared at the weapon I held in my soaked right hand. Keeping my eyes open required too much exertion, so I scanned the messy apartment one last time and then closed my lids to welcome the darkness and finality.

The bottle felt warm, gorgeous, and nourishing. Hell, it seemed like the sole way to mitigate any of the pain. Feeling the plastic numbed my loneliness. My friends and people who loved me understood neither my condition nor my state of mind. Nobody, in my skewed opinion, could help me. I was by myself and without redemption.

I was standing alone on the shore while everybody I knew embarked on a ship headed one-way to a new world.

All I could do was clutch the rope that had once held them close to me. My mind was my world. Population: one.

The painkillers removed that feeling of drowning on my brain.

I tilted the bottle toward my chin and emptied a handful of pills into my mouth. I don't remember how many I took. They danced around my saliva for a few seconds before I swallowed them all without any external liquid assistance. As I wiped the blood from the corners of my lips, the cacophonous sounds of "Amazing Grace" resumed.

"I once was lost, but now I'm found."

I can't be sure how much time passed before I fell asleep.

A bright purple light blinked through my imagination, and then all color disappeared.

My next memory is from eight o'clock the following morning. I woke up as an insult to any reasonable olfactory system. Pools of perspiration infiltrated every one of my bodily crevices, and my sour breath produced a deathly odor. Was I dead? Was I smelling my own rotting corpse? Would they have to peel me off the floor? Maybe I'd been wrong not to believe in the afterlife.

I don't think I desired death. Many of the pills I thought I had swallowed lay on the ground. I hadn't consumed enough of them to kill myself or necessitate hospitalization. Using Tylenol instead of a more lethal toxin meant I wasn't serious about dying. Maybe Tylenol should sponsor this chapter: "Tylenol: It won't kill you, even if you think you want it to."

The first thing I did the next morning was check my email. I had numerous junk messages, one of them from a penis-enlargement company and another from a Nigerian prince offering me access to fortunes. The only email I didn't delete was from Darko.

"How are things?"

This email wasn't Darko's way of keeping me as a client. He had more clients than he had time to accommodate them all. I was confident Darko had sent me messages throughout the school year because he cared about me. I viewed him (and still view him) as a big brother.

I replied to Darko's email and then forced myself to shower, dress, eat three almonds, and walk to class as if I were about to fail a Breathalyzer test. The frigid Kingston air slapped my face and reminded me of the previous night. I took a deep breath and staggered to class.

CHAPTER 27

A Weighty Death

My mindset shifted from a romantic fascination with death to overwhelming shame about the harm that a successful attempt would have inflicted upon my family. For the next week, my dreams took place in a reoccurring location: Benjamin's Park Memorial Chapel, a Jewish funeral home that is part of a two-company oligopoly in the Toronto market. They are the Google of Toronto Jewish funeral homes.

The funeral was scheduled for the present, yet as my friends entered the chapel, I saw that their appearances had reverted to what they'd looked like when I first met them. Together, these friends stood in front of the guestbook at the entrance of the chapel. Their eyes looked down at the blue carpet and then up at the natural light outside. Ari removed a razor blade from his pocket.

"Here's to our friend, Jake," he toasted in his high-pitched voice.

"Here's to Jake," about ten other friends repeated.

They passed the razor blade around, each cutting a small incision in his or her index finger and then signing my guestbook with blood.

In the mourners' room, Mom, Dad, Maddie, Nana

Sheila, Bubby Pearl, Zaidy Jerry, and Zaidy Paul were trying to console each other.

"It's my fault. I should have never let him live all on his own. I knew he was in pain, but I didn't know what to do!" Mom cried as she dropped to the floor.

"Don't blame yourself," Nana Sheila said with her arm around Mom's shoulders. "Please, don't blame yourself. That's a really horrible thing to do to yourself."

"I could have done something else. The last time I saw him, he was so skinny, so deathly looking. I knew then that I should have pressed harder, done something differently," Bubby said.

Nana Sheila and Zaidy Paul hugged Bubby, embracing her in a silent absolution that she would never accept.

"There was an interview with Christopher Hitchens on TV the other night," Zaidy Jerry said. "He had this huge vocabulary and wit—like Jake. I could have seen Jake in that kind of interview. So much potential gone. Wasted."

"Thrown down the drain," Dad added.

"I'm sorry," a staff member at Benjamin's said, interrupting. "It's time to go."

He opened the room's door to a curtained area of the chapel. In Judaism, mourners may privately view the body before the service. My family requested this viewing.

An elderly man in a black suit, white dress shirt, and gray tie watched over my casket, reciting psalms to safeguard and comfort a spirit in which I didn't believe.

The staff member opened my light maple-polished casket, revealing my body, which was lying on top of a white cotton interior. I was a peaceful corpse, dressed in the traditional shroud and prayer shawl. The panic and dread that had swamped my tormented face a few days prior had receded into expressionless calm. Death had drained my physical form of all its pain and terror. My cold hands rested on the heart that had beaten so wildly.

"Oh my God," Mom wept as she kissed my shoulder. "Oh my God."

Dad didn't say anything; he just stood over the casket as if he were hoping a miracle would bring his boy back to life. His firstborn, the vibrant boy at whom he had not long ago cranked squishy baseballs from a plastic bat, was about to become a permanent resident of the dirt. He put his head against my motionless chest and cried.

"Jake. Please, no. Please."

Tears and mucus spread across his face, rolled into his mouth, and drenched his black suit jacket. He was sobbing like a hysterical child.

Zaidy Paul rubbed the back of his son's head. Nana Sheila clutched Dad's hand, her body shaking with his constant convulsions.

"I love you," Nana said into my left ear. "Why'd you have to do this to us? We're all dead now."

One by one, they kissed my forehead a final time. Maddie was last in the procession. Before her lips reached my lifeless skin, she paused to address my corpse.

"You were the best big brother I could have asked for. I know I can't say, 'Rest in peace,' because you hate that expression. I won't say it. But, Jake, why'd you leave me? You could have talked to me more. Anything. I would have done anything for you. I wish you'd gotten help or something. My life won't be the same without you. Nothing will be the same. It's all downhill. I love you."

Maddie collapsed to the floor, where she buried her head in her knees and sobbed until Zaidy Jerry helped her stand up.

"Okay," the Benjamin's employee said.

He closed the casket and locked the box in which I'd soon decompose.

The curtain opened, exposing the mourners to the thousands of spectators who'd come to watch this display of depression.

After the rabbi connected my life to biblical verses, Maddie eulogized me.

"I never liked public speaking, but Jake always told me I should give it more of a try, so I'm doing this for him. I can't speak for more than a minute. I really just can't. I've lost my brother, my tutor, my mentor, and my best friend. I don't know how to carry on. As the days and years go by, maybe I'll be able to tell you more about Jake and all of the memories we had together, but right now, I can't say anything else other than I will always love you. I love you, Jakey."

The ritual moved graveside, where my pallbearers marveled at how light my casket was.

As the cantor sang "El Male Rahamim," a Jewish funeral prayer with a haunting, requiem-like sound, my family cried into tissues and each other's shoulders. "El Male Rahamim" was another reminder of the ceremony's finality, the coalescence of musical notes signifying ultimate termination.

The gravediggers, who wore track pants, work boots, and baseball caps, were indifferent to the sadness. They were desensitized to the endless scenes of death. Lowering me into the ground was one of a hundred tasks for which they were compensated. I was a forgettable number and would become more obscure with each passing hour.

Participants lined up in front of a mound of dirt, waiting to help fill the grave.

Amid the radiant sunshine, mud crashed against my casket until it disappeared into eternal invisibility.

When I awoke from these dreams, I felt regret. How could I have been so selfish? How could I have even contemplated ruining my family?

"Don't think about your family," the Anorexia God said after my seventh funeral dream. "Ignore all of that noise."

"No, I will not listen to you on that one."

"Use something more lethal than Tylenol. Screw your family. Once you're dead and buried, you won't see their pain. Try again now."

"What kind of evil God are you?"

"Evil? I'm the damn reason you've turned your life into something meaningful. How dare you call me evil! Go fast for five days."

"Fuck off."

"Make it one week."

"No, I'm not listening to you anymore. You are finished. You are done. I will not obey you. I don't owe you anything."

"You owe me everything, Jake. Cool down. Take a few deep breaths. Once you calm down, you'll know that I'm here for you and that you're being impulsive because of a bad dream."

I exhaled. "What do you want from me?"

"I want what's best for you, Jake."

"That's all? Then why do you want me to die so badly?"

"I thought that was the best course for you. It's possible I was wrong."

"Yeah, you were wrong."

"I'm sorry."

"I'm sorry too."

"Can we move on from this?"

"Yeah, I will do what you want. I will fast. I will cut calories. I will stay in bed for days. But please promise me you won't ask me to kill myself. The anorexia is about me, not anybody else."

"I'm sorry, my friend. I pushed you too far this time. I won't ask you to do that again. You have my word. Are we okay?"

"We're okay."

"I love you, Jake."

"I love you too."

My recovery didn't have a tipping point. I didn't suddenly remember an idea as if I were a fictional detective solving a crime through a eureka moment. Nonetheless, when I awoke from my funeral, I doubted my expression of mutual affection. I had loved the Anorexia God because I couldn't love myself. The deity highlighted my flaws and convinced me that it was the sole salvation for an otherwise unsalvageable beast. If I wanted to delay my funeral, I'd need to learn self-acceptance. I would have to recognize my positive characteristics and undermine the premises of my eating disorder. I ripped a sheet of paper from the blue pad I'd used for my goodbye note. "List of Positivity," I wrote at the top. For more than an hour, I tried to think of something to scribble as my eyes lost themselves in the paper's dizzying lines. Finally, I wrote, "You are compassionate." *There must be a contrast conjunction*, I thought. "You are compassionate, but …" My mind was like a clogged toilet that needed just one more flush to overflow with waste. I knew I couldn't pull the handle; I had to begin the process of unclogging it. Needing a distraction from the negativity, I sent a text message to my friend Ari. He and I reminisced about high school hijinks for more than an hour.

"Do you remember in grade six when you and Joel Marcus used to go around and yell at people who weren't getting the best value for their grocery purchases?" I asked.

"Classic. We were classic."

I laughed quietly.

When I put my down phone, I added another item to my list.

"You have great friends."

I fell into a nightmare-free sleep.

CHAPTER 28

WuDi Wu

Late March 2011

WuDi, the Queen's Debating Union's 167th president and my dual friend and mentor, invited himself over to my apartment. He'd told me he wanted to talk about a few things yet wouldn't hint at the subject matter. The Anorexia God worried that this persuasive intruder was going to attempt to turn me against my eating disorder.

"He's a debater," God said. "Debaters are good at convincing people to agree with them or to do things."

"You know, I'm a debater too, so I'm not that easily persuaded."

"Nonsense. You're a novice. WuDi is in fourth year. He's a million times better and smarter than you are."

"Don't worry about me. I'll be fine."

The setting sun peeked through an opening in my living room curtains.

I glanced at the blue paper I'd written on a few nights earlier. Aiming to overcome the negative voice in my head, I added to the list. "You are persuasive," I wrote. "You are a good essay writer and public speaker." As soon as I dropped the pen, I heard a knock. WuDi let himself in through the unlocked door, poured a glass of water for himself, and sat down beside me on the couch. I hadn't eaten in almost two days and was too exhausted to greet him.

WuDi studied my face for a few seconds before putting his arm around me. "Jake, what's going on with you?" He tapped my head three times. "You know I'm worried about you."

"You know, I'm not eating much. But everything's fine. I promise." I blinked nervously.

"I don't believe you. You're not well. What are you doing? What's the end goal of this?" WuDi asked.

I pressed my index fingers up against my temples and inhaled. "It's obvious I'm not well. We both know that. But I can't figure out how to stop my descent. I'm worried that—"

"I'm going to give you some harsh advice. Don't take it the wrong way. I'm telling you because I love you and want you to get better and want everything to go well."

"I know. Continue."

"You're going to kill your family. You're their son, and they're obviously horrified at what you're doing to yourself. They can sense the danger that you're in."

"You're right, but it's not that easy."

"Of course it's not. Still, if you can't get better for your own sake, use them as inspiration. Get better for them."

"I've been trying."

"Then you could put in more effort. Have you really been trying hard enough? Answer honestly."

"Probably not."

WuDi leaned his head on the cushion and looked up at the ceiling before gazing back at me. He sipped his water while adjusting the ring on his finger. "Look, I see big things for you and not just in debating. You could make something of yourself, but you need to deal with life better than you have been. You can make yourself get better. I can worry about you. Katherine can worry about you, which she does. And we could beg you to get better as much as we want to. But it's up to you. Do you want to do this to your family? Do you want to give up on a life with promise? If that's what you want to do, then you're being kind of selfish and also pretty stupid. Don't be that person. You also don't want to develop a reputation as someone who either is really depressed or can relate to others through a gutty sense of humor and nothing else."

"What do you mean by that?"

WuDi paused for almost a minute, closed his eyes, and coughed. "I mean, there are some debaters others don't want to be around that much. You're not that guy right now. But if you continue like this, you'll be that guy. Your interactions with others are often doing things like making fun of people's religions or making some sort of offensive joke. That's not always bad. There's definitely a place for funniness. That said, you have so much more to offer, and I don't want it to get lost in your attempts to always be the funny guy, you know? You could be much more well rounded and make people really want to be with you. I see that in you, and I know a lot of people who agree with me. Still, there are others who misunderstand you. Don't let them do that. In general, I guess you need to calm down a bit. Take some deep breaths, and let the world come to you a bit more. You don't always have to control a situation."

"You're right. I haven't told anybody this yet, but I tried to kill myself by swallowing a bunch of Tylenol pills."

His stoic expression didn't change. "When?"

"It was last week."

"And what happened?"

"I passed out and woke up the next morning."

"Did you go to a hospital?"

"No."

"Do you want to go to a hospital? Do you need to go to one? Do—"

"No, I feel fine now. That wouldn't do much."

"Do you think you're going to try it again?"

"No, I don't anticipate ever doing that again. I had a messed-up dream about the whole thing last night, and without giving you every detail of it, I'll just say that death isn't appealing anymore. You don't need to call some sort of hotline for me. Besides, if I were planning to off myself, I wouldn't talk about it with you. That would be strategically silly."

"Okay, then look, the same thing I've been telling you is still legit. You have the capacity to make your situation way better and to realize your potential. Go for it. Don't let this disease derail your life, Jake."

"You're right."

"I know I'm right." WuDi tapped my head twice.

"I really want to follow your advice. I want to listen to you and to live and be happy and rescue my family from the demons that are killing me. It's really hard."

"Yes, it is hard. Life isn't always easy. I've said what I wanted to say. It's your call, but I believe you can do it."

We both lifted ourselves from the couch and hugged. Ten minutes after he'd arrived, WuDi left.

"So," the Anorexia God said, "don't listen to any of that."

"He has a point," I said. "Maybe this illness isn't really accomplishing much for me."

"You couldn't be more incorrect. Don't be irrational. Look how much weight you've lost and how much more you could lose. You have a long way to go, Jake."

"Life isn't all about weight loss."

"How many times do we have to discuss this? Weight loss is a by-product of control. Life is about control. Weight loss is the best way to gain that control."

I was skeptical of his position. If control meant that moving from my bed to the coach was challenging, then perhaps the goal was futile. I conceded that suffering accompanied control, but I asked myself why I was suffering. What was the goal? For what was I being a martyr? Why couldn't I enjoy my time on earth instead of struggling in the name of a cause with elusive promises?

While WuDi had rattled my faith, I wasn't sure which voice I found most compelling. Maybe I needed to become a more dutiful anorexic, further immersing myself in the teachings of the Anorexia God. Or perhaps WuDi was correct about the edicts being a false consciousness.

I had to pick the voice I wanted to heed. Both WuDi and the Anorexia God were competing for my mind, leaving me to adjudicate the debate.

"Screw everything WuDi was babbling on about," the Anorexia God said.

Two hours after he left, I walked to a restaurant a few minutes from my apartment.

"Don't go in there," the deity in my head said. "Don't even contemplate it."

"What if WuDi is right?"

"He's not. He's—"

"What if you're wrong? I've considered giving another lifestyle a shot and coming back to you if it doesn't work."

"Wow, that's a nice way to treat somebody you love. 'Oh, sorry, I'm going to jump into the sack with somebody else and see whether I like her better than you.'"

"We're not lovers."

"I'm your partner. I matter most."

"Go to hell."

"All right, you cocky, ungrateful son of a bitch, go into the diner. Go ahead. Do it. I dare you."

I stood in front of the restaurant, its beige wooden sign and neon lights inviting me into its house of sin. To me, all of the patrons looked obese. The fatties were filling their massive faces with calories they didn't need. I focused on a man who appeared to be my age. He was eating chocolate ice cream from a ceramic bowl and quaffing a milkshake.

"If you go in there, that could be you," the Anorexia God said. "Ice cream and milkshakes are gateway drugs."

"I wouldn't eat ice cream. I'm not crazy. Gateway drugs aren't a thing."

"For you, they're a thing. And who knows what you'd permit yourself to do once you stepped in there? You might have a tiny piece of white bread, and all of sudden, you're banging down the most fattening things on the dirty menu."

"I want to have a salad."

"Salad is great. Make yourself a salad at home. Don't get it from a restaurant, because you can't control the ingredients they put in their dressings. They're usually loaded with calories."

"Can't I treat myself once? I'm tired and don't want to make my own salad."

"Gateway drug. Be smart, son."

The neon lights of indulgence were hypnotizing me. "I think I'm going in."

"No, you're not."

I took one step toward the door and looked back up to the sky. The man reached for another scoop of ice cream, half of which landed on his orange sweater. I moved back three steps.

"Give up," the Anorexia God said. "Go home. You're not going in there."

"I am. I just need a bit of time."

It was as if I were submerging one of my toes in a frigid lake, vowing that I needed a few more minutes before I pushed myself off the ladder. Maybe my savior was correct about the dangers of eating at a restaurant. Would flirting with secularism draw me away from my religion? Did I even want to be a member of this fanatical belief system of one? Would the water be too cold? I moved a few inches closer to the door, pausing my sprinting thoughts to watch the vapor exit my mouth. The freezing wind stabbed my face.

"I am going to eat at this restaurant. I can do this."

"I'm not stopping you."

I tiptoed into the vestibule, where I smelled fresh apple pie. The Anorexia God was silent, daring me to defy his rigid instructions. I felt as though I were inspecting the *Mona Lisa* after breaking into the Louvre in the middle of the night. Somebody must have been close to arresting me. The authorities had to be nearby. But I heard only indecipherable conversations and clanging kitchenware. Whether I entered the restaurant would depend on corporeal instincts rather than intellect. I could have told myself *Goddamn, I am going to eat at this place*, yet my body would not take me in the right direction. The face on the door's window was harassing me, its smile mocking the dilemma in which I was trapped.

"Excuse me, sir," an unrecognizable female voice said while someone tapped on my shoulder. "Would you mind moving?"

"Moving where?"

"You're blocking the doorway."

Apologizing, I scurried to a corner so that the woman

and her family could find a table where they would consume a meal unquestioningly.

"Jacob," the Anorexia God said. "Go home, my friend."

I glanced at the clock on my cell phone: 9:22 p.m.

I'd been waiting outside the diner for more than an hour.

"Go home."

"Sorry, mister," said a hostess who was passing through the vestibule en route to her cigarette-smoking zone. "Are you going to get a table?"

I paused. Would my body allow me to say yes?

"No, sorry. My date stood me up."

I hurried into the wicked winter and staggered down the icy sidewalk until I reached my apartment. My uncovered hands and ears were numb from the depraved air, its temperature disagreeable to my anorexic physique. I crumpled onto my bed and covered my aching head underneath a scrunched pillow.

"I can't do it!" I cried to the Anorexia God. "You're right. I love you."

"Stay with me, Jake. I will guide you toward the way. You're defying WuDi. You're staying with me and winning. Good work, Jake."

Before I fell asleep, I ate one pickle. I wasn't ready to leave my religion, for the unknowable consequences of renunciation were terrifying. If anorexia were divine, then disbelief would mean trading the prospects of infinite rewards for perpetual hell. If my convictions were false, then the net loss of absolute obedience would be minimal. This was an anorexic's version of Pascal's wager. My life seemed so valueless that the net loss, a euphemism for death, was minimal. I would not swallow a bunch of pills again, but I was content to let the eating disorder kill me.

The Anorexia God's proclamation of victory over WuDi appeared accurate—and not in a "Mission Accomplished" banner on the USS *Abraham* sort of way. I knew that WuDi was right about the selfishness of self-imposed death, but food continued to horrify me. The stability of my actions didn't reflect the instability of my beliefs.

Unsuccessfully, I tried to add an item to my list of positivity.

CHAPTER 29

The Golden Calf

April 2011, Three Weeks after WuDi's Visit

As spring warmed the campus, I hibernated in my apartment. I'd missed ten days of classes because I was too weak to sit up for more than a few minutes. My head ached from a semipermanent attachment to a gray IKEA sofa.

Getting up from the sinking cushions necessitated using all my energy stores. At least once daily, I vomited blood. While the acid burned my throat, the bathroom sessions were most malicious to my back, its muscles frail from emaciation and total dormancy. The convulsions that wrenched me toward the toilet—or the floor—made me feel as if they were shredding my spine and ripping my neck from my upper back.

I shivered in the fortress of pillows and blankets under which I buried myself. No matter how many sweaters I wore or how high the mercury on the thermometer climbed, I was cold. I wondered whether these were my last weeks. Would dying be this painful, or would it numb my body before shutting it off? I knew how to stop myself from becoming disabled, yet I was frightened of eating anything other than a handful of calorie-free vegetables. I also realized that the macho attitude toward death I'd expressed after my discussion with WuDi was internal bravado. The process of reaching nonexistence was petrifying.

I drowned out my cognitive dissonance by devoting entire days to sleeping and listening to cassette tapes from my childhood. Reliving some of my favorite childhood songs diverted my mind from the nasty spiral unfolding in my grimy cave. I closed my eyes to forget about the imminence of anorexic culmination and take my imagination back to gentle yesterdays.

On a sunny Thursday afternoon, the ritual failed.

The images that were supposed to flood my consciousness didn't emerge. I remembered dancing nude to Jewish music, but I could not visualize the scene. The anorexia had trapped me in the present, removing my visceral nexus to the soothing little boy I used to be. I pondered whether I was losing the control I presumed my religion had given and would continue to give me. Did this shelter have an escape option? Had I lost the capacity to re-create the past? I ran to the washroom and threw up blood into the yawning bowl.

"I need to eat a full meal," I told the Anorexia God.

"You do not. Embrace the finality."

"I can't remember the past."

"That's fine. You're creating something new today."

"I need this connection. Anorexia doesn't comfort me as the past does."

"Stop reliving what's happened before, and start focusing on the obstacles in front of you now."

My thoughts departed from my loss of nostalgic fantasies when I recalled that I had two exams the next week. I love exams. I love trying to predict what teachers and professors will ask. I love when they surprise me with unexpected questions. I love memorizing names and years that I can drop to flaunt my knowledge. I love the adrenaline rush of the time crunch. I love working through complex intellectual puzzles. Most people call this fascination masochistic. They think I must also pay prostitutes to tie me to bedposts and punch me until I'm unconscious. The truth is, I'm just a nerd.

I knew that being unable to remain sitting for prolonged periods would make my exams impossible to write, which was an unacceptable sacrifice. Even if I had begun consuming a reasonable number of calories, my body would not have been prepared to sit in an exam hall for three hours. This inability to undertake an intellectual challenge represented an intolerable lack of control.

I worried I was going to fail my exams because of the anorexia. It was poisoning everything. My relationship with the Anorexia God was far from healthy. Maybe, I thought, that was on me, and I needed to take a further leap of faith. After all, I'd made many new friends during the year. I wasn't sure they'd have been interested in me had the anorexia not made me more confident than I'd ever been. However, if I was too sick to enjoy the friendships, then I wasn't sure how much more value I could extract from the eating disorder.

For a few minutes, I hated the Anorexia God. I wanted to end our affiliation—until the panic about what I'd be on my own set in. I wished I could detest my eating disorder and throw it away. But I was too scared to break free. Following the Anorexia God didn't seem to be a choice. I couldn't fight the beast that had reduced me to a skeleton holed up in my apartment.

Exams were out of the question. I was going to have to email my professors to inform them I was too ill to finish my courses. Dr. Silver had already emailed me a note to excuse me from exams.

A hair fell into my eye, so I grabbed a handheld mirror from the countertop above my head and held it half an inch away from my face. Every one of my features—from the drop of perspiration to the crinkled forehead—was repulsive. I loathed not my appearance but the God particles that had metastasized inside of me. They threatened my dominion over myself, invading with a force so potent that I worried about the possibility of never reestablishing proper order. I wanted to kill the monster that I still loved.

"You're so weak. I'm your sovereign."

I slammed the mirror against the bath's ledge. The glass landed in and bounced out of the tub, sprinkling the tiles with its sharpness.

"Shut the hell up. I don't want you anymore."

Shoeless, I stood up and cut my feet on the demon that I'd tried to demolish. I crawled to the kitchen, where I ate three baby carrots.

"You're not going to have anything else," the Anorexia God said.

"Oh yeah? Watch me." I tore open an expired avocado and devoured it without cutlery. "I'm so sorry," I said. "I'm truly sorry."

"You have disappointed me."

"I can't do this anymore."

"Believe in yourself."

"I'm so sorry. I don't want to die."

I called Mom to tell her I was unwell and emailed my professors to arrange deferral of my exams. I would not admit I was mentally ill, so I said I had a serious flu bug. It wasn't really deceiving, for both Mom and I knew the origins of my sickness.

"I'm coming out there tomorrow. I need to see what's up," she said.

I washed the blood from my feet.

The next day, Mom exhumed me from the filthy apartment in which I would not die. I insisted I was all right on my own, yet my protestations were unconvincing.

"This has to end now," Mom said during the car ride home.

"What are you talking about? What has to end? I have the flu. That's all it is."

"I may not be as smart as you, but I'm not an idiot, Jake. I'm pretty swift."

I wanted to disclose everything—the fasts, the Tylenol incident, the agony that boiled within me. She needed to meet the Anorexia God, but I had to protect her from knowing the scope of my pain.

Besides, divulging what I thought was a weakness would have been awkward. I was supposed to be invincible, our family's rational voice who would advise Dad not to curse at the television when his favorite hockey team surrendered a goal and Mom not to feed white pasta to the dog. Explicitly revealing my vulnerability, I concluded, would undermine my parents' admiration for me, even if they would not confess to such a change.

I denied reality.

"I am not anorexic. Where are you getting all this from? I have a little flu. Throwing up has led to some moderate weight loss. What's all the fuss about?"

"Moderate weight loss? Moderate? Are you kidding me?"

The motionless car on the congested highway strangled me with the barrage of Mom's questions. I slouched back in my seat and hoped the road would open, easing the suffocating grip on my drained mind.

"No, I'm not kidding you. You're really exaggerating the amount of weight I've lost. I'll go see Dr. Silver about this flu to make sure it's not a serious virus, but I don't expect him to find anything unusual. It's one of those things I have to fight through. My immune system will take care of it."

"What immune system? You probably have nothing left to fight off a flu or cold. It's not one of those things. Sorry, but I'm not buying it. I've made you an appointment with Dr. Silver for tomorrow morning. I'm taking you."

"I'm busy tomorrow."

"Busy with what? You can hardly move."

"I have to study for exams," I lied.

"Ha. Exams? Fat chance that's happening."

I tried to distract Mom from talking about my already determined absence from exam halls.

"Did you hear that Brazilian waxing is out? I read it in a magazine somewhere. And here I was, all this time, ripping off every follicle just so I could wear my bikini to the beach and take it off to show the neighbors," I said. "I guess invading Iraq is in today."

"Aw, it's a shame you wasted all your money on that. Is butt waxing still okay? Invading Iraq? I don't get it."

"You'll get the Iraq connection soon. Think of presidential names. And I'm not sure about butt waxing. I'll have to research that and get back to you."

"You do that. More importantly, you need to eat. I made you an avocado salad at home, and you're going to eat it. Will you tell me why you haven't eaten this year? What's going on that made this happen? I have a right to know. I'm your mother. You can tell me."

"Nothing is happening. This is why I don't like coming home. You all drive me crazy and pretend I am so sick, when all I have is a little flu. If I sneeze, uh-oh, I must have chlamydia. It's not like I have a mental illness and tried to kill myself. You've got to stop this. It's the flu."

"How can I stop? Do you enjoy looking like this? Do you think it's nice? Jake, when people see you, they're horrified. It's like a skeleton walking down the street. You would never try to kill yourself, would you?"

"No, that would be a cowardly thing to do. Suicide is not cool."

"Are you sure? Were you ever touched inappropriately as a kid? I need to know if you were, and we could get help for that. I'm really trying to understand you."

"Yes, my teaching assistant in fourth-grade Mishnah class had a thing for me. I was convinced that we were in love and that she was going to marry me once I was old enough. Oh, how I long for her. What is wrong with you? Of course I was never touched as a kid. Do you really think I could have hidden that at such a young age? What are you seeing that I'm not? Who is feeding you—huh, pun—this information? I'm not anorexic. I'm not suicidal. I'm not crazy. You're being totally obnoxious, Mom."

I felt evil for yelling at my distraught mother, yet every time I contemplated full revelation, the God particles replaced those thoughts with a defensive insolence that preserved my sense of control.

"I'm going to have to monitor you and make sure you're eating enough. This has gone on long enough. I'm sure Dr. Silver will have some advice to give you. You'll have to listen to him."

I didn't want to insult Mom further, so I pretended to sleep for the last hour of the trip. While we were both silent until the car pulled into the driveway, I could hear the exasperation in Mom's breathing.

CHAPTER 30

Lucky Pierre

Dad was pallid. There I was, his firstborn, standing in the doorway and poking through a light blue hoodie that used to fit snuggly. He glanced at me and then moved his eyes away, as if he couldn't bear confirming the veracity of the reports on my health. "This is not a joke. How could such a smart kid do something like this? I really don't get it," he said.

Dad walked to the kitchen and grabbed a handful of almonds. I stayed in the doorway.

"I'm not sure what you're talking about," I said, dropping my knapsack to the ground. "I just have a bit of a flu bug."

"Like I said, this is not a joke."

I heard charging footsteps and barks coming from downstairs.

Our housekeeper and family friend, Anna Joy, had opened the door leading to the basement. Molly bolted up the stairs and greeted us with her typical shrieking. She ran in circles; jumped on me, scratching my chest with her trimmed nails; and shrieked until I gave her a treat. Her knees soon gave out, and she had to catch her breath on the hardwood floor.

I poured a glass of water from the sink and made my way to my room upstairs, where I lay down on my bed. Molly followed right behind me. She plunked down beside me and put her left paw on my knee. Molly usually abhorred cuddling, but I think she sensed that I wasn't right—or she thought I had food in my pocket. (If only she'd known I was anorexic.) Her rotten breath was the best thing I had smelled all year.

"Can I get you some avocado salad?" Mom yelled from downstairs.

Molly was snoring.

"No, thanks. I'm a bit nauseated from my flu."

"Bullshit!" Dad called from his room. "You're going to eat some avocado salad. Like I said, this is not a joke."

"You love saying, 'Like I said,' don't you? I'm not hungry."

Mom ignored my untruths and brought me a large bowl of her finest culinary creation. The subdued green avocado, bright red tomatoes, finely chopped purple onion, and drizzled olive oil looked damn appealing. I wanted to devour it without hearing from the Anorexia God, but before I even lifted the spoon, the vicious voice pounded my head.

"We've been over this before. Avocado is not okay. It's a banned substance. Ask for an apple instead."

"You know what? I'm done with you right now. I need to be with my family."

With surprising ease, I finished the entire serving. I was terrified of gaining weight and losing control, but for the first time in months, I didn't regret eating a meal. I wish I could explain why that happened. Why did my mindset turn? My theory is that blending my parents' terror with my physical sickness and inability to write exams produced a disdain for anorexia. The rituals and doctrine were losing the war for my mind. I was determined to learn to abandon my savior. Like a CD Walkman, the anorexia would become obsolete.

Anytime its message sneaked into my thoughts, I'd have to remind myself that there was a better alternative.

I asked Mom for more avocado salad.

Early the next morning, I was back at Dr. Silver's office, this time without the pomp and circumstance of diagnosis day. I felt ashamed that I needed medical attention for attempted self-destruction when there were people fighting against diseases that threatened lives they wanted to live. I didn't have cancer, wasn't a war hero, and hadn't been shot.

The British nurse's accent didn't sound as melodious as it had before. "Jacob, please follow me" came across as harsh and cold, a veiled suggestion that I was exiting the thrill of impending death and returning to banality. She recorded my new weight and height, measured my blood pressure, and instructed me to lie on the table in the room with zebra pictures.

I blocked the Anorexia God's comments from overtaking my mind by remembering a story about when Molly was a puppy. My parents and I had noticed reddish spots on her stomach. We thought she'd developed a severe skin ailment and took her to the vet the next day. Since my dad always assumes the worst-case scenario, he concluded that the spots were cancerous.

"Jesus, that's it. She has cancer," I overheard him say to my mom before we left for the clinic.

The vet burst out laughing almost immediately upon examining Molly.

"There's nothing wrong with her," the vet said. She was trying to subdue her laughter. "Molly is—"

"So what's wrong with her? What's that on her stomach?" I asked.

"Those are her nipples."

"So not cancer?" I said.

"Nope, just her nipples."

I also came up with lyrics for an anorexic reimagining of "I'm a Little Teapot":

> I'm an anorexic,
> tall and thin.
> Here is my ribcage;
> here's my one chin.
> When I get all triggered,
> I will cut,
> fast for days, and shrink my gut.

That memory of the vet and my new song left me internally giggling on the table when Dr. Silver entered.

"Jacob, what's new?" Dr. Silver was measured. Neither his voice nor his demeanor indicated anything dire.

"Oh, you know, I'm just snorting cocaine and shooting up heroin—the usual."

"How was your year at school?"

"Good. I did well academically and improved at debating, so all in all, I'd say it was successful."

"How was it outside of academics? Your mother has expressed concerns about you, and frankly, Jacob, seeing the amount of weight you have lost in a very short amount of time, I'm concerned too."

My weight chart on his computer looked as if it showed Enron's stock price after the turn of the millennium.

"Well, that was a bit of a problem. As we talked about last year, I'm anorexic."

"Did you see someone at the clinic in Kingston?"

"Yeah, it didn't work for me. I wasn't ready to get better then."

"Are you ready to get better now? I need an honest response."

"I hope so."

"Look, Jacob, I'm going to breach confidentiality here and talk to your mother. This can't go on. It's very serious. You've lost an incredible amount of weight in less than a year. We're not at the point of hospitalization, but if this continues any longer, we'll need to have that discussion. Do you want to talk to someone?"

"No, that's not for me. I want to do this on my own."

"I really think you'd benefit from some therapy. I'll send in a referral to a clinic for one. It's ultimately your choice, but I'd advise you to do it."

"Okay."

I was adamant about recovering on my own and ignoring the referral.

"What would you recommend I eat?" I said. "I'm not going to leave here and guzzle down three thousand calories a day. I'll have to work up to that."

"Right. You'll want to eat calorie-dense foods, such as peanut butter, almond butter, avocados, nuts, seeds, or, really, anything that tempts you, Jacob. At this point, we're looking for steady weight gain."

Steady weight gain?

The Anorexia God was clearing his blocked throat, trying to get something out and protect his interests. "Jake, are you out of your m—"

I kept telling myself to think about the Molly nipple story. I would ground myself with a distraction.

Dr. Silver requisitioned a blood test and restated the

importance of instant self-transformation. "I'm going to talk to your mother about this so she understands what's going on and can make sure you stay on track, Jacob."

I agreed, this time honestly.

"I'm going to get better," I said to Mom when I met her outside of the building. From what I would "get better" remained unspoken.

I intended to keep that promise. The Anorexia God had sapped me of my control. It was destroying everything in its path, including my family. I'd arrived at the inevitable choice of whether to live or to die. I was beginning to see my value, and most important to me, I couldn't ruin my family members' lives.

The whizzing cars and blaring horns again exemplified my inconsequentiality relative to the world. This time, my obscurity and irrelevance didn't bother me. I was happy to rid myself of the incessant yearning to be significant.

"We'll get through this together," Mom said.

Later that day, I had visitors. My four grandparents came by to see me buried in blankets and stuck on the couch in our living room.

Zaidy Paul showed me all the magic tricks his new phone could perform and introduced me to Lucky Pierre. (I apologize to whomever Zaidy stole his joke from.)

"Now, there was a man named Lucky Pierre. Ask me how lucky he was."

"How lucky was he?" I said.

"I'll tell you how lucky he was. He was so lucky that the first time he golfed, he got a hole in one. He was so lucky that anytime he bought a lottery ticket, he won the jackpot.

He was so lucky that he could swim in a lightning storm. Anyway, I saw Lucky Pierre in the changing room at our country club and noticed he had cuts all over his ass. I said to Lucky Pierre, 'What happened?' He replied in his thick French accent, 'Well, I was making love to a woman, and a chandelier fell on my ass and cut it, monsieur.' So I said, 'Lucky Pierre, I guess you aren't so lucky after all.' He said, 'Oh no, au contraire, monsieur. Had the chandelier fallen a minute earlier, it would have landed on my head.'"

Nana Sheila pretended to be angry before laughing.

Zaidy Jerry, who had spilled a quarter of a Fudgsicle on his gray button-down shirt, was oblivious.

"What was your favorite part of the year?" Bubby said.

"If I had to pick a favorite part of the year, I'd say it was probably the food at Queen's. It was top notch."

Fifteen seconds later, Zaidy Jerry joined the conversation. "Oh, Jake, tell me—what was your favorite part of the year?"

"Jerr, he just answered that." Bubby sighed. "Pay attention."

Bubby, as usual, was planning ninety-four-course meals to serve in July and August. "Okay, when we have the Wergers, Kerzners, and Sverskys over, I'll make gazpacho. The Birnbaums like that too. What do the Shermans eat? Should I have thirty-six or thirty-seven side dishes for the Singers?"

Dad was blathering on about the need to stretch before crossing the street, lest you risk a back injury. Mom was reprimanding Dad for providing unwanted advice. Maddie was complaining about school. "Like, why do I have to read a book by some dead guy? Who cares about T. William Fitzgerald or whatever the fuck his name is? Ach. Like, really. I don't need any of this shit. It doesn't matter. *The Great Gatsby* is so fucking boring."

I received a text message from Uncle Steve, who, despite his seniority, has always been one of my closest friends: "Watching the Boston Bruins just shows you how pathetic our hockey team is. What a disgrace the Leafs are."

Being home made the mammoth scoop of almond butter I was eating on the couch taste guiltless. The anorexia was wilting. I made a mental note to write, "Your family would do anything for you," on the list of positivity.

"If people didn't care about you this much, we wouldn't be so upset about what you're going through," I recalled Maddie telling me. She was right. I reasoned that since my pain was other people's pain, they had to care.

"You're worthy enough that people care about you," I added to the mental note.

My anorexic mindset had not melted completely; I tried to avoid removing my shirt near mirrors and looking down at my belly, as the results upset me. However, I was close to recovery.

One evening near the end of the summer, the Anorexia God lambasted me for eating two servings of avocado salad. We were at the cottage. I left the table during a family dinner and went to my bedroom.

"What are you doing with your life? Take off your shirt, and see what you've done. Everything we've tried to do together is now gone. We have to start again. You don't care about yourself."

I removed my "Fuck you, you fucking fuck" T-shirt to see a belly that was no longer flat. For a minute, I distracted myself from my bodily failures by reminiscing about the story of how I'd acquired the T-shirt I'd just taken off.

I was a preteenager in Florida with Zaidy Jerry. We were at a print-on-demand T-shirt shop. I noticed that design in the window and was adamant that I had to have it. Zaidy Jerry approached a man in the store.

"Excuse me," he said. "I'd like to purchase the 'Fuck you, you fucking fuck' T-shirt for my grandson." Zaidy Jerry pointed to me. "How would I go about doing that?"

The man scrunched his forehead, turned to Zaidy Jerry, and responded, "I don't work here."

Eventually, Zaidy Jerry found a store employee and bought me the T-shirt in an adult's large.

I laughed inside before returning to the subject of my horror. There was a small roll, an imperfection that frustrated me. I pinched the flab and sat down on my bed to examine how much fat would spill over my basketball shorts. At most, there was a quarter inch of an unwanted surplus. "When I start working out, I'm probably going to lose this. If I don't, I don't. Maybe that's my natural appearance. I think I am okay with that."

"Okay with that? Don't be stupid, Jake. Think with your head, not your belly."

"I'm not interested in what you have to say. Sorry."

My belly disgusted me, yet I left my room and went out onto the deck at our cottage. Both sides of my family gathered around a small outdoor table. Trevor was my one cousin there.

Zaidy Paul raised his glass to propose a toast. "Here's to the girl who wears the red shoes. She smokes all my dope and drinks all my booze. She lost her cherry, but that's not a sin because she still has the box that her cherry came in."

Nana Sheila faked irritation. "Pauuul."

"Sheil. Here's to the girl who lives on the hill; she won't do it, but her sister will. So cheers to her sister."

"Pauuul. There are kids here. Come on."

"That's cool. I've heard much worse before," I interjected.

"Shit, cocksucker, fuck, shit, fuck head, tits, fuck, tits."

"My friend, how do you know about tits?" Zaidy Paul said.

"I saw one of them on the History Channel."

"Very good." Zaidy Paul giggled. "Here's to it. Here's from it. Here's to it again. If you ever get to it to do it, do it, for you may never get to it to do it again."

"Paul, how's the golf game coming?" Aunt Bonnie asked.

"My friend, it's like wine. I get better with age. These are my golden years."

"Yeah, yeah," Uncle Dave said, eating a handful of potato chips. "Just keep him away from behind the wheel of a car."

"Or off of water skis," Aunt Karrie added while checking the data on her step counter.

"I'm ready to go skiing," Zaidy Paul said. He pulled a knee brace from his bag. "Who's going to take me?"

"Paul," Zaidy Jerry said, "you and I are far too old for that now. This is a young person's world."

"Too old? The other night, I met a couple of cute twenty-year-olds at the bar, and I can tell you that if Sheila weren't around, they would have come to my place for some jam-dab cookies and card tricks. I could have shown them Rocky the Raccoon."

"What would you think about that, Sheila?" Bubby said as she cleared plates from the scene.

"They could take him."

Dad was ranting about marijuana. "These kids smoke too much dope. It's bad. Don't you get into that, Jake.

Preserve your brain cells. Your mind is too important for that kind of stuff."

I ignored Dad's rant and instead moved to the lawn to play catch with Trevor, my first cousin and boyhood friend. Within two minutes, he threw the ball into the bushes, ending the game. We walked a few feet to the lake and talked about the past.

"We also fed Maddie mud. That was pretty hilarious too," I said.

"And she ate it. What a loser."

"Yeah, your mom was so pissed. You lost fruit-punch privileges for the rest of the night."

"Well, yeah, we fed mud to a little kid. What the hell was wrong with us?"

"We were dipshit lunatics, Trev. Man, we were such dipshits. I also convinced you to *gai kaken oifen yam*. You want to do it again for old times' sake, Trev?"

Gai kaken oifen yam is Yiddish for "go shit in the ocean."

"You're disgusting, Jake."

"I know you want to do it."

"You're gross."

"Let's at least get matching bikini waxes. What do you say we go for Gaza Strips? We'll take them out for a night on the town. Are you in?"

"Yeah, I'm in."

I rubbed my right palm across my face and felt some stray hairs, one of the few things that had changed in that timeless place. Underneath the pink sky, Trevor and I laughed until Bubby called us in for dessert. My smile was real, my laughter was unaccompanied by thoughts of impending doom, and my words were not drenched in deceit.

Had I not grown since my early years, I would have

leaped into Bubby and Zaidy Jerry's bed the next morning. As I was reviving my youth, I was growing up.

I went back to my bedroom and rummaged through my messy duffel bag to find the crumpled list of positivity. "Good people surround you," the new bullet point read.

CHAPTER 31

Lunging

Within a month, my energy and weight had increased significantly. My physical health had improved as a result. I was no longer vomiting blood, and moving had become decreasingly painful.

I was ready to work out with Darko again.

"Jacob Two-Two, welcome back," Darko said at our first session upon my return from school. "Are you ready to dance?"

"I'm so ready to dance, Darkman. Let's do this."

"You look good. You look a lot healthier," Darko said, scanning my body with his eyes.

He led me to the middle of the rubber floor and asked me to do six lunges per leg. I struggled through the exercise, but I did five of them before collapsing on the sixth attempt.

"Dude! That's awesome. Do you realize that less than a year ago, you couldn't do a single lunge? Jake, we're building something here. We're laying a foundation."

"I need to put on some muscle."

"We're going to do it. Just keep eating. But you've come a long way, my friend."

The rest of the workout was challenging without being too intense.

"Listen, dude," Darko said before I left. "You're a smart kid. You're one of these supersmart people. At the end of the day, if you put your mind to this, I know what you can accomplish. I know you've been through some shit this year. We all go through that. We have our demons. You—"

"I have been through some stuff. But I'm recovering. It's not always easy. But I'm doing it. I need to get better for everyone else."

"You need to do it for yourself too. It's not all about everyone else. You're a good kid. This is about you too."

I paused and stared at Darko's worn-out running shoes for about ten seconds. They weren't a recognizable color. "I've started writing a book about my experiences. I don't think more than ten people will read it, but I'm writing it. Maybe they'll binge-read it. That's a different disorder, but get it?"

Darko either ignored or missed my joke and looked me right in the eyes. "I know you'll write it. And when you do, you'll be one of a few people who can say they've done that. It doesn't matter how many copies you sell. You'll have put your mind to something and done it. You know how rare that is, man? Now, want to try another set of lunges, you epileptic fish?"

I shook my head. "I don't think I could do it."

"Just shut the fuck up and do it. What's the worst thing that could happen? I know you have this in you. Give me three lunges per leg for a six count."

I tried to delay the lunges. "So one of my friends told me that her grandmother introduced her to a guy who became the friend's boyfriend. I told her that the next time they're doing it, she has her Bubby to thank. Am I a home-wrecker, Darko?"

"Just shut up and do the lunges already, you sick fuck."

"You didn't answer my question."

"Do the lunges, and then maybe we can talk."

I exhaled deeply and attempted a lunge on my right leg. I allowed myself to collapse to the floor. "See? I can't do it."

"No. I don't accept that." Darko pounded a fist into his open palm. "We're not leaving here until you do this. It's all in your head. It's fucking mental, man. I can be here all day."

I exhaled deeply again and committed to refusing mental failure. "I can do this," I told myself.

I did the six lunges.

"Dude! See? You can do this."

"I can do it," I said. "We're doing it again."

We passed time by talking about the role of analytics in modern professional sports. A few minutes later, I did another set of six lunges.

"That's what I'm talking about," Darko said, slapping the side of a treadmill. "You're not even scratching the surface of what I know you can accomplish. You just have to keep eating. At the end of the day, that's the biggest thing. Keep fucking eating because you can do this."

I wanted to hug Darko.

He was the first person to address my feelings of inadequacy directly. I'd known I was academically intelligent, but I assumed I was incapable of accomplishing anything outside of intellectual pursuits. By showing me that my body could do things I didn't think were physically possible, Darko taught me I could successfully migrate outside of my comfort zone. With Darko, I learned not to submit to negativity. If I thought I couldn't do something, I'd have to first ask myself why. Could I not do it? Or was my mind creating a distortion?

I mentally applied that lesson to other aspects of my life.

Why couldn't I talk to people in large social groups? The answer wasn't incapacity. It was all in my head.

"The brain is a funny thing," Darko said, leaning against a wall beside the treadmill. "You have to stop giving up. I'm telling you right now there are so many things you think you can't do that you can actually do."

"I want to fly like a bird," I said.

Darko rolled his eyes at my smart-ass comment. "Obviously, I'm talking within reason. If you come here and say you want to bench seven hundred pounds, yeah, I'll tell you that you'd snap in half if you even looked at that weight. But the stuff we're doing here, you can do that shit, one hundred percent."

I resolved to prove Darko right.

CHAPTER 32

The Storm

I was dreaming.

A belligerent wind was sending waves onto our cottage dock. The water bounced off my bony bare feet. Underneath a dark gray sky, the whitecaps grew until they hit the shore and exploded on the concrete and steel. A storm was imminent, but without the requisite technology, you could not be sure when the weather would attack. Although it had not arrived yet, there wasn't anything calm about the scene surrounding the stick figure standing on the soaked old wood. It was the unrest before the storm, violence before more violence.

About a mile from the shoreline, a man no younger than sixty-five years old was paddling a gray aluminum canoe eastward in the opposite direction of the merciless wind. Each stroke was a rebellion against a natural world in which some little canoe was irrelevant. The aluminum thing was nothing, a pathetic dot on water that the sky could have swallowed and spit back into the lake. As the canoeist paused to wipe the moisture from his forehead, nature flung his boat back to a spot out of which he had just broken.

Other than the aluminum opening with a man inside of it, the lake was bereft of humanity. Everybody knew the clouds were going to shatter, and electricity was going to react with the water, so the canoeist was his own sole source of salvation. There was neither a god nor a person to save him from the encircling turbulence trying to flip the canoe and drain the life from its passenger. His existence depended on whether he was willing to accept the self-induced suffering that would accompany the harsh paddling that would rescue him from his mistake. After a soft thunderclap, the canoeist exerted more wattage than he probably ever had before. For him, everything was in jeopardy—every love he would have, every breath he would take, and every serene moment in which he would not be paddling his canoe. They were all at risk because he'd decided to eschew the clouds' limitless warnings. The universe was apathetic.

He moved about a quarter mile before pausing to allow his lungs to recover from their punishment. The wind reversed some of his progress, pushing him back into the pain he had overcome minutes ago.

The canoeist looked skyward and nodded, as if he were telling himself that while the final stretch would be agonizing, expending every morsel of energy in his body would keep him alive. If the beast tried to murder him, it was going to encounter a fight, the paddle strokes of a traveler who would never surrender. As the wind turned him 180 degrees, he gazed at the open water, basking in the moment and in the elements that didn't care about him.

"One. Two. Three."

He dunked his paddle in the water and fought with the unwilling water. The canoe was hardly moving, but the man's desire to live marginalized his exhaustion. He was going to paddle until either he lost consciousness or nature took away his canoe. Waves spilled over the watercraft, slowly sinking it and attempting to drown the enemy combatant.

He was now close enough to the shoreline that I could see the wrinkles on his face and the message on his tight black graphic T-shirt: "Now you're gonna get it, Bobby."

"You're so close," I said.

He didn't respond to my voice, which couldn't carry over the booming wind, yet he saw me standing on the old wooden dock. Survival was a few strokes away. Breathing like an obese pole dancer, he was still paddling at maximum efficiency, defeating the forces that would kill him if he could not escape their sociopathic fury.

When the man was, at most, five paddle lengths away from the shore, a massive wave filled his canoe with water, rendering it unusable. As the thunder intensified, he slid out of his boat and into the pugnacious pool. He would not submit to the whitecaps that worked to eliminate him.

With his head barely above the water, the swimmer front-crawled toward my dock.

"You're almost here. You're so close," I said, throwing a life buoy into the lake.

He didn't grab the ring.

The man had been swimming against the wind, but that was no matter—he was climbing the ladder to my dock.

A lightning bolt crashed against the spot where I'd first noticed him in the canoe. Roaring thunder almost immediately followed.

"Oh, I should introduce myself. I don't mean to be rude," I said. "My name is Jake."

"Hello. I'm Gantry. Your voice sounds incredibly familiar."

I handed him the dog tag that I'd kept in my pocket.

"Where did you find this?" he asked. "And how did you know it was mine?"

"I put you back together, Gantry. I put you back together."

He lifted the necklace over his head and tied it around his neck. "I feel alive again," Gantry said during the thunder's brief rest.

"I do too."

Amid the destruction, I awoke, knowing I had found salvation within my once broken mind. The encouragement of my friends and family would not change the direction in which the current was flowing. Nobody could take away the agony of recovery. Only I could regain control. I could not re-create the past, but I could correct my failings in the present and refuse to capitulate to the God whose wrath I had been living in.

I felt as if a block had opened. The positive thoughts began flowing too quickly for me to record all of them on my list.

- I treat my friends well.
- I am a good writer.
- I am funny.
- I'm a very good student.
- I think logically and reject popular narratives that don't make sense. I try to separate myself from my socialization and form my own opinions.

Unlike the first few items on the list, these replaced *you* with *I*. I was taking ownership of the abundant positivity in my life.

"Don't let these things fool you," the Anorexia God said. "These are lies."

"No, they're not. I'm a good person. I am a really good person. Nothing you say will undermine that confidence."

"Are you really sure about that?"

"Yeah, I'm absolutely sure."

The Anorexia God didn't refute my claims.

CHAPTER 33

Sinner

Lyndsay Lyons was the first friend I saw that summer. I believed she'd invited me to her house because she knew about my anorexia and felt obligated to let me vent on her couch. I was a patient. That impression was baseless, for Lyndsay had always been one of the most gracious people in my life, never requesting anything in exchange for her kindness. Though I am sure she didn't see me as a burden, I thought I was valueless. I felt that I was a chore to anybody outside of my immediate family.

"Don't let Lyndsay be another WuDi," the Anorexia God warned me before I rang the doorbell. "Keep reminding yourself that any value you may have derives from your eating disorder. Do you understand?"

"Maybe."

"If she talks to you about recovery or any of that garbage, tune it out. You can agree outwardly, yet you can't absorb it. Stay on track, Jake. Stay on—"

"Jake," Lyndsay said as she opened the door. She was wearing a white T-shirt with light gray stripes and blue jeans that fit her slim figure tightly.

"Woman."

I called her *woman* because she used the word *man* frequently.

"How's your party life?" She grinned as she tied her blonde hair into a bun. "Are you still taking shots like every night?"

"Yeah, I'm a huuuge party animal. Are you still blowing your professors to keep your marks up?"

"Shh. Like, don't tell anybody. How'd you know?"

"I guessed, but I reckon you've confirmed it now. That's one way to acquire wisdom."

"It's a big secret, man. Don't tell anyone."

"Do you know what else is a secret? Mr. Guyer and Ms. Jennings used to do it in the staff room."

"Dude, that's gross. I don't want to know that."

"Yeah, I totally made that up."

"What's wrong with you? That's dis-gus-ting."

I shrugged and laughed.

Lyndsay paused and scratched her eye before speaking again. "More importantly, how are you feeling, Jake?"

I was struck by the endued meaning that dripped from the mundane question I'd known she'd pose. People cared about me. I recognize that describing something as indescribable seems like a hackneyed cop-out, especially for a writer, but I can't give you much else. When Lyndsay asked how I was feeling, the blinding negativity subsided. Skepticism replaced my certainty of my worthlessness.

"I'm doing all right and trying really hard to get myself on track eating-wise."

"That's great. We'll have to go for dinner and, like, hang out now that we're both home. I want to hear all about your first year and the good things too. I'm not sure whether this would help, but even it doesn't, I'm always around for you."

"I know you are."

No, I didn't. I was lying again, presenting a bold facade to represent a macho confidence that didn't exist. These disguises offered me a false sense of control, a perception that I was emotionally stable during a crisis. I wanted the world to see my vulnerability, yet I had to reveal it on my terms.

"That's good," Lyndsay said. "Are you starting to feel better? Are you eating more now that you're home?"

"Yes, I'm eating more. Did you know I swallowed a bunch of pills one night?"

"You did what?"

"Yeah, I was going through a really bad time."

"Jake, you should have called me or texted me or reached out to me in some way. Don't do that again."

"I managed to get through it. Besides, I don't always want to be a burden."

"You're never a burden. I'm your friend. That's what I'm here for."

Unknowingly, Lyndsay was trouncing the Anorexia God. Every sentence reinforced that the foundational premises of my religion were faulty. My loneliness was a narrative I'd constructed irrespective of relevant facts and sustained by a severe confirmation bias. I had ignored or dismissed the relationships that could have nourished me and instead convinced myself that gloom was inexorable.

"Jake," the Anorexia God said, "you're thinking like a heretic. Don't be stupid."

"I'm not being stupid. Have you not listened to what Lyndsay is saying?"

"Yes, she has to say those things. She's doing it to appease her guilt."

"Guilt of what? She invited me here."

"Because she would feel guilty about not helping you when you've been sick."

"That's not true. We hung out before I got sick. She didn't feel guilty about anything then, did she? To believe your bullshit, I'd have to reach the pinnacle of intellectual dishonesty. You want me to evaluate myself the way an unintelligent sports fan views players, seeing solely what fits within some predetermined narrative. What sort of life is that?"

"It's a meaningful life."

"Is everything all right?" Lyndsay interrupted, noticing that I was eyeballing nothing.

"Everything is perfect. I'm just contemplating some stuff, you know. Thank you. Thanks a lot."

I don't think Lyndsay spotted the depth behind my expressions of gratitude. She couldn't have known the degree to which I was grateful for her friendship, especially given the timing. She couldn't have known she was helping me learn that I wasn't alone. She couldn't have known she was inspiring me to exorcise the toxic voice in my head and heal myself. While existence may be petrifying and finite, I was discovering that I didn't have to play the game solo.

I masked my emotions with humor.

"You know why being anorexic is really handy?" I said. "If I wanted to rob a store, I could stuff a bunch of things in a sweater without looking like the Michelin Man. That's something."

"I'm not sure if I should laugh at that."

"It's all right. We can make anorexia funny. I'm probably skinny enough that you could tie me into a figure-eight knot and attach me to a sailboat. I'd also make the perfect chimney sweep."

"You're nuts."

"You know what? Anorexics must be awesome sex partners for dominatrices—or is the plural dominatri? Hippopotami. Fungi. Dominatri. That makes sense. I'll go with dominatri—it sounds cool, woman."

My phone kept vibrating. Within an hour, four friends had sent me text messages asking me to make plans that week. One message stuck out.

One of my closest childhood friends, Mathew, wrote, "I haven't seen you in a long time. I always love being with you and miss ya, so let's hang."

I could relax in the midst of this serendipity. As Lyndsay and I spent the rest of the afternoon watching Jack Bauer violate human rights to save America from a nuclear attack, the anguish was exiting my body. My friends had reinforced the message of my dream about the canoeist. Once I understood that salvation was possible and was within myself, I could see their love. They didn't remove the pain, yet they helped me understand that its origins were fabricated. If the Anorexia God was willing but unable to prevent my anguish, then he lacked power. If he could prevent my anguish but decided against it, then he wasn't omnibenevolent. I was beginning to realize that the Anorexia God wasn't my sole companion.

That evening, I ate a second serving of dinner.

"Good morning. Did you forget about me?" the Anorexia God asked when I awoke from the previous day's high.

"To be honest, I haven't really thought about you."

"You haven't thought about me? Is that some sort of sick joke?"

"No, you're very far from my mind."

I slipped on my "May Contain Nuts" boxer shorts and went downstairs for breakfast. Mom had already prepared a bowl of oatmeal for me and was going to deliver it to my room. I surmise that people want to bring you breakfast in bed when you are recovering from anorexia. Call it a perk of recovery—or an ano sweatshop.

"Nope, you're not going to touch that. Consider it and die," the Anorexia God said.

"I'm going to eat this."

"No, you're not."

I ate the oatmeal but felt the guilt simmering in my gut. This guilt was different than what I was used to experiencing. I no longer thought eating was harmful or that it represented a lack of control. I was just so used to being anorexic that eating the oatmeal seemed wrong. The reason-based underpinnings of my anorexia had vanished.

"There isn't much protein in here. Ditto for fat. It's pretty much all carbs. This is bad. It's really bad," the Anorexia God said.

"You know, people want to see me. People like me. It doesn't matter. It's okay. I don't need you anymore."

CHAPTER 34

Solidarity

Tiffany and I had continued to talk. By the end of April, we'd see each other at least once weekly. She was too nervous to meet my parents and didn't want me in her house, so during the early part of the 2011 summer, we spent most of our time together in parking lots. Nonetheless, I thought there was a cheesy but charming quality to being the sole people in places that humanity had abandoned for the night. The open car windows would let in the sounds of distant engines and chatter, yet only our hushed voices were comprehensible.

On a rainy evening in May, Tiffany and I were sitting on a curb in a parking lot at my elementary school. A few hours earlier, Mom had offered me tickets to a live production of *Billy Elliot*, which she could no longer attend. While I wanted to invite Tiffany, I also knew she wouldn't immediately agree to a third consecutive outing together.

"I think it's important that we don't spend too much time together and become dependent on one another. Besides, I don't like you in that way right now, so I don't want to give you the wrong idea," she would tell me. "I need my own life away from you too."

Indeed, in the early phase of our friendship, talking to

Tiffany was high-stakes diplomacy. If I used the wrong word, relations between the two states would deteriorate.

"Oh shoot, I forgot to ask a friend to go to that play with me tomorrow night," I said, pretending I had already mentioned the admit-ones.

"Which play?"

"I told you about it an hour or so ago."

"No, you didn't. Which play?"

"My mom has tickets to see *Billy Elliot* tomorrow night, but something came up, so she can't go. I need to find somebody else to go with, but I forgot to do that and actually don't know any of my friends who would like to go. I may wind up going by myself. Maybe I'll scalp the extra ticket."

"That sucks, man."

"Yeah, it's too bad the play isn't another day. Then I'd invite you to go. I'm sure you're sick of me after two days in a row, so you wouldn't want to go tomorrow."

"I love musicals, so it's definitely a shame."

"And Elton John did the music for *Billy Elliot*, which means it will be great."

"Ah, that sounds like so much fun."

"You could come if you want to."

"Three days is a lot. I think that's too much."

"Meh, I promise we won't make it four."

"I'll have to ask my parents."

Every time nineteen-year-old Tiffany indicated that she needed parental permission, I was certain I had achieved my goal. We could have leaked the agreement to the media and scheduled a press conference in the Rose Garden.

I picked up Tiffany at Union Station. She was wearing a solid-black scoop-neck dress that extended about halfway down her thighs and a silver bracelet that required frequent adjustments.

"We're going to meet my family today," I informed her.

"Whaaat?"

"Yeah, I told them you were going to come by before the play. They got us tickets, and they want to meet you."

I alternated between telling Tiffany nice things about my father and teasing her by making up stories about his negative qualities. He was welcoming, I claimed, but he also had a nasty habit of unprovoked verbal outbursts. Tiffany expressed her difficulty discerning which of my statements were true.

"I'm so nervous," Tiffany said when we arrived at my house. "They're going to hate me. I know it."

I put my hand on Tiffany's shoulder and admitted that I'd lied about the negativity. She smiled and nodded tepidly. Side by side, we exited the car and approached the entrance of my house.

Dad opened the door, and Mom held the dog away from Tiffany. Molly growled and barked.

Tiffany's eyes watered as soon as Molly introduced herself. The latter looked at me as if to say, "Sorry, buddy, but my tail comes first," and the former hid behind Dad and me.

My parents and Maddie, who alternated between text messaging friends and surfacing for air, tried to maintain a conversation with Tiffany but didn't progress beyond triviality.

"It's been a really nice May," Dad said.

"Okay," I interjected. "We're going to leave for dinner."

We took a prom-like picture on the front lawn and ate a high-carb, high-calorie meal at an Italian restaurant.

Each slurp of spaghetti was uncomfortable. I imagined the noodles expanding in my stomach and blowing up the size of my belly. Recovery would require partaking in painful activities. I would have to consume foods that I had feared, even if I felt ashamed in doing so. The behavior had to precede the mindset.

"So can we get this over with and say we're in a relationship now?" I said as we walked into the theater.

"No, we're not dating. We're just friends."

"Then why are you wearing such a nice dress?"

"I wore a dress on our one date, didn't I?"

"But now we are in public, and you're all dressed up. I'm wearing fancy clothes, which I almost never do. Look at me. I'm wearing a button-down shirt."

"So?"

"So you must therefore like me."

"The sets look so pretty," Tiffany said, aiming to distract me from discussing our future. "Do you think the play will be scary?"

"You can admit that you like me. It's—"

The lights dimmed, and the play started. Throughout the first act, I tried to hold Tiffany's hand, but she rejected my attempts and, at one point, placed my right arm on my lap. Undeterred, I put my hand on her shoulder.

"Would you stop it?" she said. "I'm trying to watch the play."

Tiffany treated my hand as if it were an army attacking a village, a colonial force that she needed to repel lest it violate her knee's sovereignty. With my palms planted on my quads, I watched the last few minutes of the first act.

"I don't feel well," Tiffany murmured when we stepped into the hall during intermission. "I'm having a bit of trouble breathing." Her face had turned white, and she was holding her head. "I am really overheated."

I cut a long line at the concession stand, angering two women who were both wearing so much perfume that nobody would have noticed if they'd shit their pants.

"Hey, there's a line here, mister."

"I'm very sorry. She isn't feeling well and just needs some water. I'll be really quick."

"She can wait. It's not an emergency."

"No, I don't want her to wait."

Such a transgression was the most aggressive thing I had done since cheating on Madame Kurtz's elementary school French test. In this case, my goals were more important than the ice cream bar these women were waiting for. Tiffany was sick, and I had to improve her condition. I bought two bottles of water, one for Tiffany to drink and the other to cool her forehead.

The Anorexia God claimed that the eating disorder had caused this breakthrough. An internal debate emerged in my mind. One side argued that I would never have made such a breakthrough with Tiffany if I had weighed more than I did. The Anorexia God and I were winning together. The other side maintained that I was experiencing this success after I'd increased my intake. I was thriving on my own. The latter side's most compelling argument was that continuing to be anorexic would kill me. I'd die, and Tiffany would find somebody else.

As I handed the water bottles to Tiffany, she put her arm around my shoulders. I knew then that I no longer needed to ask if she liked me anymore. Nonetheless, I knew that her arm's position was akin to Tiffany calling her parents.

"I think I may kind of sort of maybe like you just a little bit."

"Well, all it took was a bit of nausea and overheating. Why didn't I come up with that before dinner and a documentary?"

"I don't know."

"I want to go clubbing with you and your friends," I said.

"You? Clubbing? Um, no."

"Why not?"

"Because. That's my time with friends."

"We'll talk about this another time."

"Okay, but I need my time with friends."

"I just want to go a few times."

"No. You're not invited."

"Never?"

"Dude, you're not."

I didn't debate the point, as I was just happy we were dating. I also didn't care that the perfume queens were scowling at me as noxious smoke billowed out of their ears. However, I realized I was ignoring that we were not compatible.

CHAPTER 35

Born Again

September 2011

I awoke in a sweat. My head ached, and the objects in my bedroom were floating as if gravity had disappeared. "You're disgusting. You're ugly. Look at what you are doing to yourself," the Anorexia God said.

Silenced by the unexpected return of self-destructive thoughts, the rational voice in my mind couldn't respond. I stumbled out of bed, took off my shirt, and studied my stomach in front of the mirror.

"It's ghastly. It's an abomination. You're totally out of control, Jake. Stop now before you can't get yourself back on track."

I removed from my pocket the note I'd written before the Tylenol incident. I'd hung on to the note and wanted it with me when I returned to remind me of the progress I'd made.

> To all those who care,
>
> I apologize for my cowardice. You neither deserve nor are responsible for this sordid decision.

Thank you for everything.

Love,

Jake

I breathed deeply and insulted the deity. "I'm not going to give in. You know what? It doesn't matter. I'm going to be healthy and work out, and maybe I won't be an Adonis. Maybe that's not the way my body is supposed to look. I don't care anymore."

Suddenly, Molly began gulping, indicating that she was about to vomit. I lifted the dog from the carpet and placed her on the tile, where she threw up bits of an orange rubber ball she had swallowed. Before she could re-consume what she had discarded, I scooped it up with the blue piece of paper.

"I'm never going to have to write such a thing again."

Pinching my stomach, I found fat that I had not noticed. "I don't care."

I hugged Molly and allowed myself to enjoy my liberation. She nuzzled her head into my chest and barked at me until I rubbed her neck.

As I hugged her, the puke seeped through my sunken note.

Molly lifted her head and burped in my face.

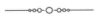

The day before I moved back to Kingston for my second year of university was the first time I knew without question that I was no longer anorexic. I had increased my caloric intake to an appropriate level over the summer, yet until that day,

I had still felt hints of guilt when I disobeyed the Anorexia God. My eating disorder provided me with such a rigid structure that ignoring it seemed wrong, even sacrilegious. Recovery was like proving to a devout monotheist that God wasn't real. Demystifying the rituals shattered my identity and interrupted my perceived purpose. I needed months to shun what once had been holy.

I remember the last time the Anorexia God in my head tried to instruct me. It was his final attempt to remain relevant, a plea to be spared from the deicide he was facing.

An almond butter sandwich smiled at me.

"Don't you dare do it," the voice said. "Don't even think about it. Almond butter? Are you crazy? Do you know how many calories are in almond butter? If you really need to eat and be such a goddamn wimp, fine. Have a cucumber. Have a tomato. Have a pickle. Have a carrot. Have a glass of water. Try some rhubarb. But almond butter? Really? Be smart, Jake. That would be like Moses telling the burning bush to piss off. Don't do that. Don't do that to me. You need me."

"I don't need you."

"You think you can accomplish anything on your own? You can't do that."

Without hesitation, I ate the sandwich, slaughtering the divine ruler I'd once worshipped and moving on from the rites that had owned me. We are not supposed to speak ill of the dead, but I gamboled over the bloody corpse of my fraudulent companion.

I reminded myself of what I'd learned with Darko. The voice that told me I couldn't do many of the things I wanted to accomplish was a distortion. I didn't need the Anorexia God. I had to approach life with the attitude that my comfort zone was not an impenetrable border.

I could sleep at night knowing I'd be excited to wake

up the next morning because I was valuable. I was in a honeymoon phase with life, ignoring all negativity, loving the present, and looking forward to the future. Home with only Molly on a late-summer evening, I danced shirtless to Ricky Martin's "Livin' La Vida Loca," shaking my puny butt to the chorus. The dog was barking at me, probably thinking her master's convulsions pointed to something ominous.

"How will I know that you will never do this again?" Dad asked me at the table, on which a small corner of the sandwich remained. "Like I said, you are going back to school tomorrow, so we really need to be sure this is not going to be a repeat of last year, you know."

"Whatever I say will come across as an empty promise," I said, licking almond butter off my lips. "I will try to look at this from a very cold and rational perspective. Let's say, hypothetically, that I lose control again. I don't anticipate that ever happening, but for the sake of this discussion, let's accept that it does. The difference between today and last year is that I have already tried anorexia. It didn't work. It was awful. What I previously thought was control was actually the utter opposite. It was a total failure—total collapse, you know. Really, I botched a year. I was too sick to do anything, and I couldn't even write exams. Anorexia is basically a 'Been there, done that' kind of thing."

"Okay, I guess we are going to have to trust you. Please just give us your word that you are going to eat. Don't do what you did last year again, okay? Be healthy, please," Dad said.

Had my parents known about some of my incidents, they might not have permitted me to move away from home as quickly as I did. Even after I recovered, I still had secrets—many of which I didn't divulge until I wrote this book.

"You can trust me. I promise that this year will be

different. I won't come home looking like a stick-figure drawing. Ramadan is over. There will be no more yearlong Yom Kippur."

The next day, Mom, Dad, and Maddie moved me back to Kingston. I sensed my parents' trepidation and understood that no matter what I told them, I would need to avoid future emaciation to support my promises. Like a criminal, I appeared probable to reoffend. However, as we drove into the university hub, I was certain my anorexia was gone. I regretted allowing myself to flee reality and spiral into a state that had almost killed both my family and me. If the pun weren't so inappropriate, I'd have said that my anorexic years made me want to throw up—wrong disorder, I know.

I returned to Kingston with a mended brain. The city had not changed, but I entered it for the first time.

I stepped into the apartment and immediately walked to the spot where I had passed out after my failed termination attempt. While the images of that night dashed through my mind, the narrative behind them changed. I was happy I had been unsuccessful, and I was ready to be reborn, not in a finding-Jesus kind of way but as a human being. Life would whip obstacles at me, yet I would fight them instead of surrendering. I didn't consider myself a prisoner anymore. The past was an architect of the present rather than a fatality worth mourning. I could watch old movies and look at childhood pictures, smiling at those enjoyable days without yearning to travel back in time. Nostalgia became reminiscence.

When my parents left me alone in my apartment for the beginning of my second year, I lay on my back in the place where somebody was supposed to find me dead and rotting. As I looked at the windows outside of which the noises of inebriated students once had tormented me, I knew that my desire for death was gone. Lying on the dusty carpet, I was born again. Although I'd gained twenty pounds, I carried less weight than I had ever carried before.

That night, I went to a house party. I wasn't the first to show up, and I didn't stand by myself in a corner. I talked to the people there without wondering whether my arm hung awkwardly.

When I awoke the next morning, I opened my eyes to embrace the light and possibilities.

EPILOGUE

Am I Still Eating?

I have been recovered for more than seven years and, since the summer of 2011, have never contemplated returning to disordered eating—unless you consider drinking green bullshit smoothies a disorder. The Anorexia God never visits me.

In April 2014, I graduated with an honors bachelor of arts degree from Queen's University. I took a year off to write this book and tutor students in how not to write. The latter involved convincing a client not to use "Karl Marx takes it up the ass" in an academic essay. I am now in my final year of law school at the University of Toronto. I'm still surprised that the Law Society of Upper Canada is going to let me become a lawyer.

I'm not sure how my industry will react to this book. But I have wanted to share my experiences with the world so that others understand they are not alone. After finishing my freshman year of university, I worked with two role models, Merryl Bear and Suzanne Phillips, at the National Eating Disorder Information Centre, where I spearheaded their first significant male-awareness campaign. With the Queen's Mental Health Awareness Committee, I revealed my story to audiences of students and professionals who wanted to listen.

I recognize that I myself will never mitigate the stigma that accompanies mental illness. Nonetheless, I hope that I can use my pain to humanize a subject that is usually too academic and that if you or somebody you know feels empty, you can find hope in me. I don't think I can offer much more beyond being a symbol, because I am neither qualified to provide nor capable of providing comprehensive advice on how to deal with an eating disorder. However, I can give a few general tips based on what I found useful.

If a person in your life suffers from disordered eating, don't dwell on his or her weight. I wanted people to tell me I was skinny—even too skinny—because it vindicated my project of attaining supreme control. You may approach the person with your concerns as long as your tone is calm and compassionate. When family members yelled at me for shunning food, they pushed me to intensify my isolation. I saw them as threats to my clandestine religion. The Anorexia God's soothing voice was always more persuasive than a collection of frantic pests. This is not to say that my parents and grandparents were wild. On the contrary, my family was loving and supportive. They could not have nurtured me to health in the midst of my darkest moments, yet once I decided to recover, their affection inspired me to expel the Anorexia God from my mind and countered my false perception of solitude.

I recommend that without an imminent threat to one's life, your primary role should be trying to ensure that the individual does not feel abandoned. You can be critical, as WuDi was, but you must be careful not to hurt an already vulnerable person. WuDi questioned the extent to which I was trying to recover and cautioned me against wasting my existence on a death trap. You can be helpful without calling a person a moron for being ano or being accepting of an eating disorder in an "Oh my goodness, your anorexia is the most amazing thing ever" kind of way. "I wish I was anorexic and stick thin like you are" is probably not an intelligent comment—and yes, I heard that twice. Locate a balance that you think is appropriate. Maddie embodied that poise. She listened. I talked to her because I trusted she wouldn't share our conversations' details with anybody. Calmly, she communicated her concerns and aimed to construct the ground floor of my self-worth. Maddie suggested external help but was unaggressive. She knew I'd have to buy into that option. I didn't want to see a therapist.

If your mind is broken, seeking assistance will not make you weak. Guys, your testicles will not fall off. My recovery without expert care indicates merely that the programs in which I participated didn't match my needs. Many talented mental health professionals have directed and will continue to direct patients toward paths of healing. Ultimately, you must want to be repaired. You have to embrace the challenge. This acceptance does not mean your journey will be linear. There may be points at which you relapse and the myriad voices in your head compete for standing. You may continually have to fight the relentless war inside your mind, losing some battles and feeling as if you will never win. Don't avoid support because you think the symptoms of your mental illness will never return. Fight them on every battlefield.

My friendships were a necessary component of my recovery. Once I no longer believed I was fundamentally different from everyone else, my social life improved. For most of my teenage years, I convinced myself that I was another species, a burden incapable of interacting with my peers. Even when I was with my close friends, I worried that I was a pest. Altering these biases was key in my recovery.

I accepted that I was quirky and, at the same time, had to work at expanding my social circle. People would not chase me. As you have read, my friendships revealed that solitude was a state of mind, a misperception that the Anorexia God reinforced. The friends to whom I have dedicated these words deserve recognition.

Though the external encouragement was constructive, the decline of my physical condition was a crucial part of my recovery. Eventually, you will break down, as you can't continually deny your body nutrients and expect to live healthily. In the end, shunning food will impound your mobility. Anorexia may appear to be the perfect companion, but it will transform into a debilitating illness. Lying on the floor while reeking of your vomit is not glamorous. Disregard the initial beauty.

Perhaps the most valuable advice I can give is that you should be silly sometimes. I believe that sporadic immaturity is a hallmark of maturity. Chuckle at stupidity. Make fun of yourself because you are fallible, and your imperfections are probably comical. I will be forever grateful to my parents for raising me in an environment with infinite mirth. We still taunt and swear at each other without malice, for our house would be dull otherwise.

My advice might be useless. Ignore what you don't deem valuable, and don't rely on me. Trust professionals over anything I've said. I've reluctantly offered my suggestions only in case you think they may work for you or someone in your life. It's okay if they don't appeal to you.

AFTERWORD

By Dr. Gillian Kirsh, PhD

Memoirs of individuals and their recovery stories abound in self-help literature. However, few authors can take the reader inside their experience the way Jacob does. Jacob shares every aspect of his experience battling anorexia: his family background, his feelings of social disconnect at school and camp, and his struggle with self-confidence during university. Given that eating disorders have the highest mortality rate of any mental health illness (between 10 and 15 percent), Jacob's story is important for sufferers and their carers. Jacob is vulnerable and unabashedly forthright and shares his story with his whole heart.

He tells his story uniquely. His razor-sharp sense of humor and intellect illustrate the perspective he maintained even while in the deepest throes of a disorder that is known to devour the heart, soul, and mind. This perspective is invaluable to parents and caregivers, who often feel completely disconnected from their loved one. The disorder is known to hijack the sufferer's reasoning abilities and perspective and, ultimately, the self, such that carers feel stymied in their attempts to work their way through to recovery. Jacob's deification of anorexia, the Anorexia God, is evidence of the way the disorder can brainwash its inhabitant into ignoring objective facts ("you're too thin; you need to eat") and giving way, like the rabbit hole in *Alice in Wonderland*, to an unending pursuit of thinness. The eating disorder's hold on the individual is powerful; Jacob's god persuaded him to believe that "beyond your anorexia, you are nothing. You have very little to offer the world. At best, you are average, a blob of meh." As Jacob says, "I thought that my eyesight must have been failing, for the filthy image that shot back at me could not have been real. The Anorexia God was right. My belly had expanded to at least ten times the size."

Jacob encourages parents and carers to continue to persuade, support, love, and not give up on their loved one.

An eating disorder is one of the most elusive mental health disorders to understand and treat. A recent report on eating disorders to the Canadian parliamentary standing committee on the status of women (November 2014) highlighted the paucity of resources for the prevention and treatment of eating disorders. Psychiatrist Dr. Blake Woodside cited "egregious discrimination" as the cause. "If there were waits like this of four to six months for prostate cancer treatment, there would be a national outcry. There would be marches in the streets. But because eating disorders affect teenage women, there is no outrage or political action." The tragedy, then, that males face is even more egregious. While historically, one in nine sufferers has been male, more recent research shows rates are increasing to as high as one in three (Eisenburg, Nicklett, Roeder, and Kirz 2011).

The prevalence of eating disorders among college men ranges from 4 to 10 percent. A recent study on a large university campus found that the female-to-male ratio of positive screens for eating disorder symptoms was three to one (Eisenburg et al. 2011).

Large-scale surveys have demonstrated that male body-image concerns have dramatically increased over the past three decades from 15 percent to 43 percent of men being dissatisfied with their bodies, rates that are comparable to those found in women (Goldfield, Blouin, and Woodside 2006; Schooler and Ward 2006).

Approximately half of individuals with an eating disorder also suffer a comorbid major depressive or anxiety disorder. Therefore, appropriate, effective, and early treatment is crucial. Family-based treatment shows promising results (with approximately 80 percent of individuals achieving weight restoration) when the illness is not yet chronic (the individual has suffered for less than one year) and at younger ages of onset (less than eighteen years old; Lock and LeGrange 2015). Average long-term success rates are about 50 percent, indicating the pressing need for innovation and improvement in therapy.

Jacob's recovery from the brink of death is extraordinary. Only when his academic survival is threatened does he see the futility of his attempts to continually restrict his eating and the paradox of control. At his lowest, Jacob was fasting, and initially, he consumed 425 calories per day (far less than the required number to maintain a minimum normal weight for his height). He was in control of his intake but had become out of control in every other aspect of his life.

Jacob offers a rare, honest depiction of what life is like with an eating disorder. He also speaks to the difficulties of growing up and accepting himself upon release from his family cocoon into what feels like a harsh reality. In some ways, it is a reality created only in his mind; in others, it is a genuine departure from the adoration he received at home, such that the contrast is inevitably stark and difficult to manage. Jacob's story is a gift to caregivers in that he shares what every parent yearns to know about what goes through his or her child's mind so that he or she can reach in and help pull the individual out of a most challenging time.

To parents and caregivers, in this book, Jacob is clear that his parents and grandparents had the best intentions as they tried to boost his self-confidence. This speaks to a larger issue in parenting today, in that criticism is frowned upon and positive reinforcement abounds. Helicopter parenting efforts are not building self-esteem. Adored and admired children are sent off to university only to realize that they are ill equipped to cope with the rigidities inherent in education and evaluation, and they end up failing and lying to their parents, wasting years and thousands of dollars.

Psychologist Dr. Alex Russell urges parents to allow for painful, noncatastrophic failures in children (see his parenting aid, *Drop the Worry Ball*). Jacob makes this point as well: we need to celebrate average so that overachieving children do not "internalize praise from their families and [fail to] understand why the outside world seems so disconnected from their homes." The overfocus on developing positive self-esteem is not the panacea to failure. Rather, we should strive for self-acceptance and resilience in the face of failure.

Success almost never occurs without accompanying failure. It is through making mistakes that we learn that we do not fall apart and that we have worth beyond our achievements. For some children and adolescents, the self-concept begins to develop around a sense of achievement when they are reinforced for being smart, diligent students. At an extreme, when these individuals go on to protect themselves against failure (i.e., avoid situations in which they may not succeed and work hard to ensure success in those in which they engage), they lose the opportunity to develop a sense of connection to their inner worth.

When self-esteem is tenuous, the reward system shifts to the sense of control and mastery that one experiences through controlling caloric intake and weight loss. The eating disorder fills a void and offers a brief reprieve from the unrelenting sadness or uncertainty about one's worth. As noted above, Jacob's disorder was most strongly related to a social disconnect. He was extremely sensitive to the possibility of upsetting others and, as he describes, a near obsession with "the desire for people to like [him]."

Jacob is very clear that he "grew up in a loving and nurturing family." In efforts to understand this puzzling disorder, many have turned to the family as a potential cause. This was clearly not the case with Jacob. In fact, his parents' concern and his need to be with his family, combined with his need to achieve academically, motivated him to turn his mind against the Anorexia God.

Jacob's story is similar to others in the main themes and trajectory of the disorder. But it is unique in that he was able to recover on his own with his family's support and without professional help. Research on the efficacy of therapy consistently shows that the relationship between therapist and client supersedes any particular modality or set of tools. Jacob reminds us of this when he states that he was seeking a human connection. The connection was also what he needed, what would comfort him more than the anorexia. It is a reminder to always prize the relationship over technique or an overfocus on symptoms and outcomes.

A striking theme in Jacob's story is a plea to families to never give up on your child. Even when Jacob was in the tightest grip of the disorder, a part of him remained open to his parents' intervention. Parents need to know that no matter how stubborn their child appears to be, he or she is suffering. Sometimes this looks like an adaptive adolescent search for autonomy. However, there is a stark difference between healthy separation and pushing away love and support in a time of need. Emotion-focused family therapy labels these as miscues: a child pushing you away is really saying, "I desperately want you to be involved."

Another valuable lesson is that in helping others recover, we do not need to get mired down in convincing them that they are thin enough. This is another trap that caregivers often get caught in. Logic and reason may have been productive in the past, but they do not have a place with anorexia. Jacob shares that it is not so simple: some awareness of thinness is there, but the allure of the pain relief and feel-good from the disorder outweighs the ability to perceive reality.

Parents need to pay attention to their own gut feelings and follow them. Many parents worry about further alienating their child. This may happen initially but is usually temporary. In the context of an open, warm, and loving relationship, every teen wants to be rescued from the intense suffering of an eating disorder, depression, anxiety, addiction, etc. Jacob says he was "trapped inside the prison of [his] mind." When the child or adolescent's mind is not functioning adaptively, it is a parent's duty to step in.

Jacob's story is a valuable resource for individuals suffering from an eating disorder, anxiety, or depression. His openness enhances our understanding of these complex and often devastating conditions. His story is also one of resilience, hope, and the possibility of overcoming a critical illness.

Printed in the United States
By Bookmasters